RIVER CAFE TWO EASY

Rose Gray and Ruth Rogers

EBURY
PRESS

Photographs by David Loftus. Designed by Mark Porter

Introduction

River Cafe Two Easy is the second volume of River Cafe Cook Book Easy. It was in Puglia last May that we mapped out the chapters and wrote in our notebooks the easy and delicious recipes we wanted to include in this, our sixth cookbook.

Over the year we had travelled to cities and regions of Italy, both familiar and new — to Verona for Vin Italy, the huge wine fair, to Milan, to immerse ourselves in the tradition and sophistication of a city that takes food so seriously, to the Cinque Terre on the coast of Liguria for a family wedding, and to neighbouring houses in the Val d'Orcia in southern Tuscany, cooking with our friends and family.

Our first chapter, Mozzarella, like the Bruschetta chapter in River Cafe Cook Book Easy, is simply a putting together of ideas using a few seasonal ingredients. All quick, easy and delicious ways to begin a meal with mozzarella.

For us, salads are simple combinations of vegetables served at room temperature – grilled, boiled, roasted, slow-cooked and raw. In this chapter, there are boiled potatoes with just anchovies and capers, fine green beans cooked until soft then mixed with lumps of local hard cheese, and an unusual toasted bread and rocket salad with olives and vinegar.

Recently in The River Cafe we have increased our range of cured meats and salamis. We have also started to use traditional smoked fish such as eel and haddock, cutting them like Italian carpaccio and bringing out the flavour with olive oil and lemon juice.

In Puglia, we found tomatoes used in practically every dish, and it was there that we decided to devote a whole chapter to tomato pasta. We have included a summery spaghetti with raw tomato and rocket, a winter pappardelle with pancetta and cream, and two recipes for preserving tomatoes.

Throughout Italy there are interesting variations combining fish with pasta. Every cook and restaurant has their own version of spaghetti vongole and we have included the versions we love – with white asparagus from Verona, fried zucchini from Rome, and broccoli from Naples.

We always have a soup chapter in our books. In this one many are meals in themselves, robust and distinctly regional. A chickpea soup we had eaten in Milan was a delicious way of cooking chickpeas with a piece of pork. In the same restaurant we found the pappardelle soup with borlotti beans. And in a trattoria in the market we had an intriguing soup of just red wine and broccoli – no bread, no herbs, but, as the chef told us, one crucial clove of garlic.

We have called our fish chapter Fish with…. . In Tuscany we ate our favourite strong-flavoured fish, red mullet, with olives and anchovies, in Puglia we were surprised to eat a kind of sushi, thin slices of raw tuna with just a piece of bruschetta and lemon, and in Liguria we loved the simplicity of boiled langoustine with olive oil and sea salt.

We nearly always cook game birds with wine, looking for flavours in a particular wine to complement each bird. This is the first time in one of our books that we have suggested the variety of grape. Some of them are international varieties but all are produced in Italy.

For the roast meat chapter we have returned to traditional recipes such as pork cooked in milk, using the fattier shoulder instead of loin, and vitello tonnato, this time spread with a concentrated tomato and basil sauce or a strong mayonnaise flavoured with anchovy rather than tuna.

The flavour of the grill on meat and fish is very Italian which is why we have put them together. Grilling on a barbecue outside in the summer is quick and easy. It is all about simplicity – you take a fish, bird or steak and either marinate or brush it with olive oil using a rosemary stick.

From the beginning, our passion for vegetables has been at the heart of The River Cafe. The first thing we do when we arrive in Italy is to find the local market, which perfectly reflects the season and the region. As every Italian cook has many recipes for the same vegetable, we too have included more than one way of cooking zucchini, porcini, potatoes and aubergines. All are easy

and rely on the quality of the vegetables.

The last three chapters of the book are devoted to puddings. Baking fruits is a way of concentrating their flavours. We use a lot of vanilla, cinnamon, ginger and different types of sugar, a style more River Cafe than Italian.

Lemon juice, lemon peel, and lemon essence feature frequently in the breakfast cakes, granitas, and cheesecakes we enjoy eating when in Italy. The lemon, ricotta, pinenut cake comes from a pasticceria in San Casciano, the vodka granita, from the bar of The River Cafe and the very, very easy lemon almond cake is similar to the ones served in the cafes on the autostrada.

We end the book the way we like to end a meal – with chocolate and coffee and those rich, indulgent cakes that we know everyone loves to eat. A bitter mousse cake, a hazelnut chocolate cake, and a boozy version of tiramisu.

Every now and again in River Cafe Two Easy, we have put in a more ambitious recipe. Killing a live crab may be something you have never done, and cooking a beef shin for twelve hours or a chicken for four may seem excessive but it is in this excess as well as in the simplicity of these recipes that we find the pleasure and excitement in cooking. We hope you enjoy these easy recipes as much as we do.

Rose Gray and Ruth Rogers

All the recipes are for four except where mentioned. The cakes and tarts are for eight to ten.

1

Mozzarella

Beetroot, tomato, capers
Raw zucchini, prosciutto
Broad bean, olives
Bruschetta, tomato, olives
Grilled aubergine, roast tomato
Salami, cannellini, olives
Asparagus, rocket, Parmesan
Summer herb, crème fraîche
Red and yellow peppers, capers
Grilled fennel, prosciutto
Marinated anchovy, spinach
Celery, radish, Parmesan

Beetroot, tomato, capers

Boil the beetroots until tender, then peel and slice into 5mm discs. Slice the plum tomatoes into similar discs. Wash the salt from the salted capers, and drain. Mix the capers with red wine vinegar and olive oil. Combine the tomato and beetroot together, season, then stir in the capers and juices. Place on the plate with the mozzarella, and serve with torn-up basil leaves.

Raw zucchini, prosciutto

Using a Y-shaped potato peeler, shred the zucchini into fine ribbons. Mix lemon juice with some olive oil, and season. Toss the zucchini in the dressing, adding a few rocket and mint leaves. Place on a plate, add the mozzarella, and lay slices of prosciutto over.

Broad bean, olives

Boil the broad beans until tender. Drain and season, add stoned small black olives. Toss the rocket and mint leaves with lemon juice and olive oil, and season. Tear the mozzarella into four. Put the leaves on the plate with the mozzarella. Sprinkle over the olives and broad beans.

Bruschetta, tomato, olives

Cut the tomatoes into quarters and squeeze out the seeds and juice. Mix together with basil and olive oil, and season. Stone the small black olives, mix with black pepper, dried chilli, lemon juice and olive oil. Grill a piece of sourdough bread on both sides, then lightly rub one side with garlic. Season and pour over olive oil. Place on the plate with the olives, tomatoes and mozzarella.

Mozzarella

Grilled aubergine, roast tomato

Cut plum tomatoes in half lengthways, and remove the seeds. Season with salt and pepper and drizzle with extra virgin olive oil. Bake in a 200°C/Gas 6 oven for 15 minutes. Slice an aubergine into 1cm discs, and grill on both sides. Toss with basil, olive oil and lemon juice. Season and place on the plate with the tomatoes and mozzarella.

Salami, cannellini, olives

Drain and rinse a tin of cannellini beans, and gently heat with lemon juice and some olive oil. Season and purée. Stone the small black olives, and toss in a little olive oil. Finely slice the fennel salami, and place on the plate with the mozzarella. Put the bean purée alongside, and scatter with the olives.

Mozzarella

Asparagus, rocket, Parmesan

Cook asparagus for 5 minutes in boiling salted water. Drain, toss with olive oil and season. Toss the rocket leaves with lemon juice and olive oil and mix with the asparagus. Add shavings of Parmesan.

Summer herb, crème fraîche

Boil chard leaves until tender, then drain, cool and roughly chop. Dress with olive oil and lemon juice, and season. Slice the mozzarella into 1.5cm slices, and place in a bowl. Add crème fraîche, seasoning and a few crushed fennel seeds. Roughly chop a little fresh basil, parsley and mint, and lightly stir into the cheese mixture. Place on the plate with the chard, and drizzle with olive oil.

Red and yellow peppers, capers

Wash the salt from the capers and drain. Grill a red and yellow pepper until the skins are blackened. Peel, remove seeds, then tear lengthways into quarters. Toss with olive oil, red wine vinegar, torn basil, capers and black pepper. Place on the plate with mozzarella.

Grilled fennel, prosciutto

Slice fennel lengthways into 1cm pieces, and boil until just tender. Drain and dry on a cloth, then grill on both sides. Toss rocket leaves in olive oil and lemon juice with the grilled fennel, season. Place on a plate with slices of prosciutto and the mozzarella.

Marinated anchovy, spinach

Boil spinach leaves until tender, drain and cool. Wash and fillet the salted anchovies, add pepper, then squeeze over lemon juice. Mix lemon juice and olive oil together, season. Toss the rocket leaves and, separately, the spinach, then combine. Mix the greens together, and place on a plate with the mozzarella. Put the anchovies over.

Celery, radish, Parmesan

Wash radishes and some of their leaves, then slice finely. Use the pale heart of celery. Finely slice the stem and keep a few of the leaves. Shave the Parmesan. Mix lemon juice with red wine vinegar and olive oil and season. Toss together the radish, celery and celery leaves in the dressing. Place on the plate with the mozzarella. Place the Parmesan shavings on top and drizzle with olive oil.

Mozzarella

2

Salads

Borlotti bean, sweet potato

Fresh borlotti beans	1kg
Plum tomato	1
Garlic cloves	2
Sage leaves	2 tbs
Sweet potatoes	500g
Dried chilli	1
Dried oregano	1 tbs
Ex. v. olive oil	

Preheat the oven to 210°C/Gas 6.

Pod the borlotti beans. Peel the garlic. Put the beans in a saucepan, cover with water, and add the garlic, tomato and sage. Bring to the boil and simmer for half an hour or until tender.

Peel the sweet potatoes and cut into 3cm pieces. Crumble the chillies. Put the sweet potato in a bowl with the chilli, oregano, and 3 tbs olive oil. Season and toss. Place a piece of foil in a baking tray, and lay out the sweet potato in one layer. Bake for 20 minutes. Turn the pieces over and bake until tender and crisp on the edges.

Drain the beans, remove the sage, garlic and tomato skins, return to the saucepan, and add 3 tbs olive oil. Season. Mix the beans and sweet potato together, and serve warm.

'We use fresh borlotti for salads in the summer, but dried beans are delicious as long as they are less than a year old. Look for borlotti di Lamon, which have a creamy texture. Simmering, rather than boiling, helps keep skins intact. Let the beans cool in the saucepan in their cooking liquid to keep them moist. Add salt only at the end of cooking or the skins will toughen and crack.'

Potato, capers, anchovy

Waxy potatoes	750g
Salted capers	3 tbs
Anchovy fillets	12
Fresh red chillies	2
Lemons	2
Ex. v. olive oil	
Rocket leaves	100g

Peel the potatoes. Rinse the capers. Split the anchovy fillets in half lengthways. Cut the chillies in half lengthways, scrape out and discard the seeds, and chop. Halve the lemons. Squeeze the juice of ½ lemon over the anchovies.

Cook the potatoes in boiling salted water until tender. Drain and cut each potato in half lengthways and in half again lengthways. Place in a bowl, and add the capers and red chilli whilst still hot. Squeeze over the juice of ½ lemon, and season. Pour over 4 tbs olive oil and toss gently.

Roughly chop the rocket, season and toss with ½ tbs lemon juice and 2 tbs olive oil. Add to the potatoes, and scatter the anchovies over.

Serve with lemon.

Potato, green bean, tomato

Waxy potatoes	500g
Plum tomatoes	12
Green beans	250g
Red wine vinegar	2 tbs
Ex. v. olive oil	6 tbs

Peel the potatoes. Cook in boiling salted water until tender. Drain and whilst still warm, cut into 1cm slices. Skin the tomatoes (see page 66). Cut in half lengthways and squeeze out seeds and juices. Top and tail the green beans and cook in boiling salted water until tender, then drain.

Combine the vinegar and olive oil and season.

Toss one-third of the dressing into the beans, another third into the tomatoes. Season both. Mix the remaining dressing with the potatoes and season. Toss the beans, tomatoes and potatoes gently together, and serve.

Radicchio, walnut, Gorgonzola

Radicchio head	1
Fresh 'wet' walnuts	500g
Gorgonzola	300g
Parmesan	100g
Lemon	1
Ex. v. olive oil	

Remove the tough outer leaves of the radicchio, cut the head in half, and then shred into ribbons. Crack open the walnuts and remove the flesh from the shells. Cut the rind from the Gorgonzola and cut into fine slices. Shave the Parmesan. Squeeze the juice of the lemon.

Mix the lemon juice with 4 tbs olive oil, and season.

Put the walnuts in a bowl and stir in half the dressing. Toss the radicchio ribbons with the remaining dressing, then add the walnuts and Gorgonzola slices. Lightly toss, then put on individual plates, and cover with the Parmesan shavings.

Serve with olive oil drizzled over.

'Gorgonzola is a blue-veined cow's milk cheese made in Northern Italy – the longer the ageing, the stronger the flavour. The piccante is a harder-textured, strong-flavoured cheese that works well in this traditional combination of walnuts and bitter radicchio. The creamy, mild dolcelatte is delicious used in sauces.'

Toasted bread, olives, vinegar

Ciabatta slices	4
Rocket leaves	100g
Small black olives	4 tbs
Fresh red chilli	1
Garlic clove	1
Ex. v. olive oil	
Red wine vinegar	2 tbs
Thyme leaves	1 tbs

Preheat the oven to 220°C/Gas 7.

Cut the crusts off the bread. Wash and dry the rocket. Stone the olives. Split the chilli in half lengthways, remove and discard the seeds, and finely chop. Peel the garlic.

Put the bread in a roasting tin, drizzle with olive oil and toast in the preheated oven for 5 minutes. Turn over, drizzle with a little more oil, and cook until brown, another 5 minutes. Rub the toasted slices on one side with the garlic.

Combine the red wine vinegar with 6 tbs olive oil, and season. Put the olives in a bowl with the chilli, thyme and 1 tbs olive oil.

Break up the bread, and put in a bowl with the rocket. Toss with the dressing. Add the olives.

'We vary the dressings for salads depending on the ingredients. With this salad of bread and olives use red wine vinegar rather than lemon juice as it has a sweetness and sharpness that goes well with the olives.'

Chicory, ricotta, prosciutto

Chicory	250g
Young spinach leaves	250g
Lemon	1
Ricotta	200g
Ex. v. olive oil	
Prosciutto slices	8

Break the leaves off the chicory. Remove the stalks, wash and dry the spinach. Squeeze the juice of the lemon.

Mix the ricotta in a bowl with a fork to break it up. Add half the lemon juice, 3 tbs olive oil and season.

Mix the remaining lemon juice with three times its volume of olive oil.

Put half the spinach leaves in a bowl and dress with the lemon dressing. Lightly mix the remaining spinach leaves and chicory with the ricotta sauce. Add these leaves to the other leaves, and gently toss.

Serve with slices of prosciutto draped over.

'Chicory has a distinctive bitter taste and the family includes Belgian endive, radicchio, catalogna, scavola and the wild version, dandelion. Catalogna, a less well known variety with long, pointed green leaves, is the most bitter. Use the tender hearts and small leaves in this salad. We cook and use the larger outer leaves like spinach.'

Savoy cabbage, capers, parsley

Savoy cabbage	**1 small**
Salted capers	**2 tbs**
Flat-leaf parsley leaves	**4 tbs**
Red wine vinegar	**2 tbs**
Ex. v. olive oil	

Discard the tough outer leaves of the cabbage. Cut the cabbage in half and remove the core. Slice the cabbage very finely. Rinse the capers in a sieve under a running tap. Chop the parsley.

Make a dressing with the red wine vinegar and four times its volume of olive oil. Season.

Toss the cabbage with the dressing. Add the parsley and capers and toss again.

'A jar of capers in salt is one of the essentials of the Italian store cupboard. Use them in sauces such as salsa verde and dragoncella. Both salted capers and those preserved in vinegar should be rinsed well before using. The smaller salted capers have the most intense flavour.'

Green bean, Parmesan

Fine green beans	500g
Parmesan	75g
Lemon	1
Rocket leaves	100g
Ex. v. olive oil	

Top and tail the green beans. Grate the Parmesan. Squeeze the lemon. Wash and dry the rocket.

Combine the lemon juice and three times its volume of olive oil and season. Reserve 2 tbs, and mix the rest in a warm bowl with the Parmesan.

Cook the beans in boiling salted water until tender. Drain, immediately add to the bowl with the Parmesan, and toss well. The Parmesan will melt and coat the beans. Season well.

Toss the rocket with the reserved dressing. Place on plates with the beans over, and serve.

'Estate-bottled extra virgin olive oil should have the name of the producer, the type of olives, the area where they were grown and the year of production on the label. We buy Tuscan oils pressed from the Moraiolo and Frantoio olive varieties which are picked early giving the oil a fresh olive flavour, spiciness and strong green colour. As olive oil ages, it loses its intense flavour. We use young oil to pour over bruschetta, soups, salads and vegetables, and older oil for cooking.'

Green bean, mustard

Fine green beans	500g
Lemon	1
Flat-leaf parsley leaves	3 tbs
Dijon mustard	3 tbs
Ex. v. olive oil	

Top and tail the beans. Squeeze the juice from the lemon. Chop the parsley finely.

Cook the beans in a generous amount of salted boiling water until tender, not al dente.

Put the mustard in a bowl. Stir in the lemon juice and then very slowly add olive oil until the consistency is of mayonnaise.

Drain the beans thoroughly and add to the mustard sauce. Toss with the parsley, check seasoning, and serve whilst still warm.

'When combining mustard in the dressing with vegetables we use a surprisingly large quantity of Dijon mustard. In this recipe its smooth texture mixed with olive oil becomes a mayonnaise-like sauce.'

Cucumber, mint, mascarpone

Cucumbers	1½
Mint leaves	2 tbs
Fresh red chilli	1
Mascarpone	250g
Crème fraîche	5 tbs
Ex. v. olive oil	
Lemon	1

Peel the cucumber, cut in half lengthways, remove the seeds. Cut in half again and into 5cm lengths. Chop the mint. Wash the chilli and finely slice on the diagonal. Squeeze the lemon juice.

Combine the mascarpone and crème fraîche, and season well.

Combine the cucumber and mint with the lemon juice and 3 times the volume of olive oil, season.

Serve with mascarpone and the chilli sprinkled over.

'Look for cucumbers that are unwaxed. They should be firm and rounded to the ends. Avoid any with withered, shrivelled tips or ones that bulge in the middle as they are likely to be filled with large seeds.'

Crab, fennel, tomato, radicchio

Crabmeat	500g
Fennel bulbs	2
Radicchio head	½
Lemons	2
Dried chillies	2
Flat-leaf parsley leaves	2 tbs
Ex. v. olive oil	
Plum tomatoes	4

Remove the tough outer leaves and stalks from the fennel. Remove the tough outer leaves from the radicchio. Squeeze the lemons. Crumble the chillies, and chop the parsley.

To make the salad, finely shave the fennel bulbs into a bowl. Finely slice the radicchio into the same bowl. Slice the tomatoes across as thinly as possible. Let any seeds and juice drop out. Add to the bowl.

Mix the lemon juice with four times its volume of olive oil, and season. Use half this dressing to dress the salad, and mix the remainder into the crabmeat (see note) with the chilli and parsley.

Serve the salad with the crabmeat alongside.

'If you buy live crabs, kill them just before cooking. Put them in boiling salted water for 8-10 minutes according to size and pick the meat whilst the crab is still warm – it will be easier to get the meat out of the shell. If you buy crabmeat, get some of the brown meat too and serve a spoonful of each per serving.'

Salted, smoked & dried fish & meat

Bottarga, mâche salad

Bottarga	200g
Cherry tomatoes	250g
Mâche leaves	300g
Lemon	1
Ex. v. olive oil	

Wash the tomatoes and cut in halves, or quarters if larger than 2cm in diameter. Wash and dry the mâche. Squeeze the lemon.

Mix the lemon juice with three times its volume of olive oil, and season.

Put the tomatoes and mâche together in a large salad bowl, season and toss with the dressing. Immediately shave the bottarga over and mix in. Use a potato peeler to get fine shavings. Drizzle individual portions with extra virgin olive oil.

'Bottarga is the name given to the sun-dried roe of the grey mullet. Sardinia is where the fattest grey mullet are caught and where most bottarga comes from. Bottarga is sold vacuum packed in its natural form which is two fish roes joined. Some bottarga is dipped in wax to preserve its moistness.'

Salted, smoked & dried fish & meat

Smoked haddock carpaccio

Smoked haddock	600g
Fennel seeds	1 tbs
Lemons	2
Ex. v. olive oil	

Crush the fennel seeds. Squeeze the juice of 1 lemon, and cut the other into wedges.

Using a long, flat-bladed knife, slice the haddock as thinly as you possibly can along the length of the fish.

Arrange the slices to cover each plate. Sprinkle with black pepper and the fennel seeds. Drizzle the lemon juice over and then sprinkle each plate with 1 tbs olive oil.

Serve with a wedge of lemon.

'The smoked haddock for this recipe should be the Finnan haddock from the east coast of Scotland. Small haddocks are split open, the heads removed but the bones kept in, lightly salted in brine and then cold smoked to a pale, straw-yellow colour. Avoid bright yellow fillets of large haddock as their flavour is too strong for carpaccio.'

Salted, smoked & dried fish & meat

Anchovy, bruschetta, butter

Salted anchovies	8
Dried chillies	2
Lemons	3
Sourdough loaf	¼
Ex. v. olive oil	
Rosemary sprig	1 large
Unsalted butter	100g

Prepare the anchovies as in note. Remove the spine bones and heads. Crumble the chillies. Halve the lemons. Cut the bread into 4 slices.

Put the anchovy fillets on a flat plate with the juice of 1 lemon, black pepper and dried chilli. Drizzle olive oil over.

Grill the bread, rub with rosemary, then butter generously. Lay the anchovies on top.

Serve with lemon.

'As these anchovy fillets are used whole, it is important to buy anchovies preserved in salt; those preserved in oil are more suitable for mashing or chopping. To prepare, rinse the anchovies under a slow-running cold tap to wash off residual salt. Carefully pull each fillet from the bone. Discard the head and pull off the fins and tail. Pat dry and use immediately, or, to keep, squeeze lemon juice over and cover with olive oil. This bruschetta makes a great savoury breakfast.'

Salted, smoked & dried fish & meat

Smoked eel, celery, capers

Smoked eel on the bone	**500g**
Celery heads	**2**
Salted capers	**50g**
Dried chillies	**2**
Lemons	**2**
Ex. v. olive oil	

Pull off the tough green stalks of the celery and keep for other use. Cut the heart in half lengthways, wash, and then finely shave, keeping a few of the tender pale leaves. Rinse the capers. Crumble the chillies. Squeeze the juice of 1 lemon, and quarter the other.

Mix the lemon juice with three times its volume of olive oil. Season and add the chilli. Put the capers in a small bowl, add 1 tbs of the dressing. Mix the celery with the celery leaves and remaining dressing.

Skin and slice the eel, and divide between 4 plates. Add the celery salad and scatter with capers. Serve with lemon.

'Look for eel sold with the skin intact as it will be fatter and juicier. The belly should be yellow and the back brown. Fat eel is definitely good eel and the skin will peel easily.'

Salted, smoked & dried fish & meat

Smoked eel, samphire

Smoked eel on the bone	500g
Samphire	400g
Lemons	3
Fresh horseradish	100g
Crème fraîche	150ml
Ex. v. olive oil	

Skin and slice the eel, and divide between 4 plates. Sprinkle with black pepper.

Pick through the samphire, cutting off any tough stalks. Wash thoroughly. Squeeze two of the lemons. Cut the other in quarters.

Peel and finely grate the horseradish. Mix with ½ tsp sea salt and the crème fraîche. Add 2-3 tbs lemon juice.

Cook the samphire in boiling water for 5 minutes or until tender. Drain and toss with olive oil and 2-3 tbs lemon juice.

Divide the samphire between the 4 plates. Spoon the horseradish over the samphire. Serve with a lemon wedge.

'Samphire becomes available around the end of April. It grows on the tide and is hand-picked, mostly in Norfolk, Suffolk and the Brittany coast. Samphire has fleshy stems and a fresh, salty taste. It is mostly sold through fishmongers.'

Prosciutto, asparagus

Prosciutto slices	400g
Asparagus	500g
Mint leaves	3 tbs
Lemon	1
Ex. v. olive oil	

Preheat the oven to 220°C/Gas 7.

Trim the asparagus of any woody stalks by flexing the base of the stem until it snaps. Wash and dry. Chop the mint. Squeeze the juice of ½ a lemon .

Put the asparagus in a bowl and toss with enough olive oil to lightly coat each stalk, season.

Arrange the asparagus in a roasting tin, and roast for 10 minutes.

While warm, toss the asparagus with the mint and add the lemon. Put the prosciutto on a large plate with the asparagus.

Prosciutto, melon

Prosciutto	400g	
Charentais melons	2	

Halve the melons and remove the seeds.

With a large spoon, scoop out pieces of each half melon and place on a plate. Drape the prosciutto slices over.

'Prosciutto is the cured leg of pork. The curing process and ageing, as well as the rearing of the pigs themselves, varies in Italy from region to region. The most famous prosciutto is from Parma, where the pigs are fed on whey, a by-product in the making of Parmesan cheese. Parma is sweet with a pale colour, in contrast to prosciutto from San Daniele which has a stronger flavour and darker colour. Tuscan prosciutto is saltier than most and usually cut into thicker slices. There are many other regions which make prosciutto worth trying when visiting Italy. When buying your prosciutto make sure it is not sliced too thin.'

Salted, smoked & dried fish & meat

Prosciutto, rocket

Prosciutto	400g	
Rocket leaves	100g	
Red wine vinegar	1 tbs	
Dijon mustard	1 tsp	
Ex. v. olive oil	3 tbs	

Wash the rocket carefully, and dry well.

Combine the red wine vinegar and mustard. Slowly stir in the olive oil, season.

Toss the dressing and leaves together, and place on plates in mounds. Drape the prosciutto over the rocket to cover it completely.

'Use broad-leaf, cultivated rocket in this salad; it is more tender and less peppery than wild rocket.

There are many other varieties of rocket. Turkish, Greek and Cypriot shops often sell a large-leaf rocket in bunches which has a strong peppery taste and is quite fleshy. The problem is that it doesn't keep well.

We actually grow a Turkish variety of wild rocket. This perennial bush-like plant regrows its slender leaves each time it's picked and is the strongest-tasting rocket of all.'

Salted, smoked & dried fish & meat

Mixed salami, two crostini

Felino salami	100g
Finocchiona salami	100g
Coppa di Parma	100g
Small black olives	60g
Garlic clove	1
Dried chilli	1
Tin cannellini beans	400g
Ex. v. olive oil	
Ciabatta loaf	½

Finely slice the salami and coppa. Stone the olives, and roughly chop. Peel the garlic and squash it with sea salt. Crumble the chilli.

Drain and rinse the beans. Heat the beans in a small saucepan with the garlic salt, 3 tbs olive oil and some black pepper for 2 minutes, then smash roughly with a fork.

Mix the chopped olives with the chilli and 1 tbs olive oil.

Cut 8 slices of ciabatta at an angle, and grill on both sides. Place 2 slices on each plate.

Spread one crostini with the smashed cannellini, and sprinkle the olives over the other. Arrange the mixed salami alongside.

'Salamis are made throughout Italy, but each region makes its own in a particular way – with different seasonings, textures and curing according to local customs and traditions.

The salami we love are the lean and delicate Felino, the hard, finely chopped Milanese and coppa, the sweet, cured, rolled shoulder from Parma. Buy salami in a piece and slice it yourself.'

Bresaola, Parmesan, balsamic

Bresaola	400g
Parmesan	125g
Lemons	1½
Ex. v. olive oil	
Balsamic vinegar	3 tbs

Shave the Parmesan. Squeeze the juice of the ½ lemon, and cut the other into wedges.

Mix the lemon juice with three times its volume of olive oil.

Place the bresaola over each plate. Season and drizzle with the lemon dressing. Cover the bresaola with the Parmesan shavings. Drizzle the balsamic over each plate.

Serve with a wedge of lemon.

'Bresaola is a top side of beef cured in salt and then air-dried. Like prosciutto and salamis, it should be served as quickly as possible after it is sliced.'

Finocchiona salami, borlotti

Finocchiona salami	300g
Fresh borlotti beans	1kg
Garlic cloves	2
Red wine vinegar	3 tbs
Ex. v. olive oil	
Plum tomatoes	4

Pod the borlotti beans. Peel the garlic.

Put the beans in a medium saucepan with the garlic and cover with water. Bring to the boil, then simmer until tender, about 25-35 minutes. Drain, season generously, and add the vinegar and 3 tbs olive oil.

Slice the plum tomatoes in half lengthways and then each half into 3 lengthways. Season the tomatoes then mix with the borlotti beans.

Slice the salami as finely as possible. Divide the borlotti beans and tomatoes between 4 plates and place the salami over. Serve drizzled with olive oil.

'Finocchiona is a fat, loose-textured, soft salami typical of Tuscany. Fennel seeds and garlic are combined with pork and it is then aged to develop the flavour.'

Salted, smoked & dried fish & meat

4

Tomato pasta

Spaghetti, raw tomato, rocket

Spaghetti	320g
Plum tomatoes	4
Garlic cloves	2
Dried chilli	1
Capers	2 tbs
Black olives	3 tbs
Rocket leaves	3 tbs
Ex. v. olive oil	3 tbs

Cut the tomatoes in half. Squeeze out excess juice and seeds, and chop the flesh coarsely. Peel the garlic and squash with 1 tsp of sea salt. Crumble the chilli. Rinse the capers and stone the olives. Roughly chop the rocket.

Combine the tomatoes with all the ingredients except for the rocket. Season generously, add the olive oil and put aside for 30 minutes.

Cook the spaghetti in boiling salted water until al dente. Drain, and stir the pasta into the tomatoes. Add the rocket and toss to coat each strand. Season with black pepper.

Serve with olive oil.

'Plum tomatoes are fleshy, easy to peel and have hardly any juice or seeds which makes them ideal for making rich, thick tomato sauces. This raw sauce should only be made in the summer, when you can buy sun-ripened plum tomatoes that are really sweet.'

Tagliatelle, tomato, basil

Tagliatelle	320g
Garlic cloves	2
Basil leaves	2 tbs
Parmesan	50g
Olive oil	1 tbs
Tin tomatoes	2 x 400g
Unsalted butter	100g

Peel and slice the garlic. Tear the basil. Grate the Parmesan.

Heat the oil in a thick-bottomed pan and fry the garlic until soft but not brown. Add the tomatoes and season. Cook over a medium heat for 20-30 minutes or until the sauce is very thick and the oil comes to the top. Add the basil.

Cook the tagliatelle in boiling salted water until al dente. Drain into a colander. Melt half the butter in the hot pan, return the pasta, and add the remaining butter. Toss well. Add the tomato sauce and toss well again.

Serve immediately with the Parmesan.

'Plum tomatoes, in tins or jars, are essentials of the Italian store cupboard. The best are the long-shaped San Marzano variety, preserved in their own juice. Avoid tinned tomatoes that contain purée or sauce, as this will affect the flavour of your own tomato sauce.'

Penne, tomato, dried porcini

Penne	320g
Dried porcini	40g
Garlic cloves	2
Flat-leaf parsley leaves	1 tbs
Parmesan	50g
Tomato sauce	5 tbs
Unsalted butter	100g
Ex. v. olive oil	

Soak the porcini in 200ml boiling water for 10 minutes. Peel and finely slice the garlic. Chop the parsley. Grate the Parmesan. Make the Tomato sauce (see page 62).

Drain the porcini, straining through muslin or paper towel, keeping the water. Rinse the porcini and chop coarsely.

In a thick-bottomed saucepan, melt the butter and add the garlic. Add the porcini, and fry until soft. Add a little of the porcini liquid, and simmer until it has been absorbed. Stir in the chopped parsley. Add the tomato sauce and season.

Cook the penne in boiling salted water until al dente. Drain and stir the pasta into the sauce. Toss well.

Drizzle with olive oil and serve with grated Parmesan.

'This sauce is best served with a hard pasta such as penne. It is also delicious with wet polenta. When buying dried porcini look for pale-coloured stems and light brown caps as darker pieces may be oven dried. A fresh, light porcini perfume (as opposed to a Marmite-like smell) is also a good indicator.'

Tomato pasta

Spaghetti, boiled tomato

Spaghetti	320g
Ripe plum tomatoes	500g
Red onion	1
Carrot	1
Celery head	½
Basil leaves	2 tbs
Dried chilli	1
Tin tomatoes	400g
Ex. v. olive oil	

Make a slit in the side of each tomato, put in a bowl and cover with boiling water. Leave for ½ minute then remove into cold water. Peel as soon as they are cool enough to touch. Chop the tomatoes. Peel the onion and cut in half. Wash the carrot and cut in half. Remove the outer leaves of the celery, and use the white part. Wash and chop the basil and crumble the chilli.

Put all the vegetables into a saucepan with the tinned tomatoes, season, bring to the boil, and simmer gently for 45 minutes, until the vegetables are soft and some of the juices have evaporated. Cool, and put through a mouli. Stir in the basil and chilli.

Cook the spaghetti in boiling salted water until al dente, drain and add to the sauce.

Serve with olive oil.

'To preserve tomatoes, choose ripe, unblemished tomatoes. Blanch and peel them and then pack tightly into sterilized jars and seal loosely. Bake in the oven at 200°C/Gas 6 or boil in a large saucepan for 20 minutes. Alternatively, blanch and peel, deseed and chop the tomatoes. Boil for 5 minutes and then pack into sterilised jars and hermetically seal.'

Spaghetti, boiled tomato two

Spaghetti	320g
Ripe plum tomatoes	2kg
Red onion	½
Basil leaves	2 tbsp
Ex. v. olive oil	

To make a tomato purée, make a slit in the side of each tomato. Bring a large saucepan of water to the boil and add 1 tbs sea salt.

Add the tomatoes and leave them in the water until the water comes back to the boil. Remove the tomatoes with a slotted spoon, and peel off the skins whilst still warm. Make a cut into the length of each tomato, and put in a colander over a bowl to drain off all the juices. Leave for an hour. Put the tomato pulp through a mouli. Bottle if not using immediately.

To make the sauce, peel and grate the onion on the coarse side of the grater. Chop the basil.

Put the onion into a medium thick-bottomed saucepan and cover with 2cm water. Heat gently and simmer until all the water has evaporated. Add the tomato purée and 2 tsp sea salt. Simmer for 20 minutes until the sauce is thick and sweet. Season.

Cook the spaghetti in boiling salted water until al dente, then drain and add to the sauce. Add the basil and olive oil.

'Both these tomato sauces are made without olive oil in the base. The oil is added only at the end. This recipe was given to us by the Planeta family from Sicily.'

Orecchiette, tomato, ricotta

Orecchiette	320g
Cherry tomatoes	350g
Garlic clove	1
Parmesan	50g
Basil leaves	3 tbs
Ex. v. olive oil	1 tbs
Ricotta	200g

Cut the tomatoes in half and squeeze out the juice and seeds. Peel and chop the garlic finely. Grate the Parmesan. Wash the basil.

Combine the tomatoes and garlic, season, add the oil, and toss to combine. Let marinate for 15 minutes. Put the ricotta in a bowl, season and stir.

Cook the orecchiette in boiling salted water until al dente, then drain.

Gently heat the tomato mixture and add the drained orecchiette, stirring gently to combine. Finally, stir in the ricotta.

Serve with the Parmesan.

'Orecchiette, little ears, is the pasta of Puglia. The tomatoes for this recipe should be almost over-ripe. Ricotta is tossed in at the end and coats the orecchiette, clinging to the hollows of the pasta.'

Spaghetti, tomato, green bean

Spaghetti	320g
Garlic cloves	2
Dried chilli	1
Parmesan	50g
Ex. v. olive oil	1 tbs
Tin tomatoes	400g
Green beans	100g

Peel and finely slice the garlic. Crumble the chilli. Grate the Parmesan.

Heat a thick-bottomed pan. Add the olive oil, then the garlic, and cook until soft but not brown. Add the tinned tomatoes, season, add the chilli and cook over a medium heat for 20 minutes.

Top and tail the green beans, then cook in boiling salted water until very tender. Drain well. Combine the green beans with the tomato sauce.

Cook the spaghetti in boiling salted water until al dente. Drain and stir the pasta into the tomato and green beans. Season and toss with a little olive oil.

Serve with the Parmesan.

'Vegetables, cooked until soft and then combined with thick tomato sauce, are typical of Southern Italian cooking. We were excited by this combination of green beans, tomato and spaghetti. The green beans should be incredibly fine so they will twirl around the fork with the spaghetti. In midsummer you can find fine green beans from France and Italy.'

Pappardelle, tomato, pancetta

Egg pappardelle	320g
Plum tomatoes	6
Pancetta slices	150g
Dried chillies	2
Parmesan	100g
Unsalted butter	150g
Double cream	150ml

Skin the tomatoes (see page 66), deseed and roughly chop the flesh. Cut the pancetta into 2cm pieces. Crumble the chilli and grate the Parmesan.

Melt the butter in a thick-bottomed pan, add the pancetta and chilli, and gently cook until the pancetta begins to colour. Add the tomato, season and cook gently for 10 minutes. Add the cream and cook for a further 10 minutes.

Cook the pappardelle in boiling salted water until al dente. Drain and add the pasta to the sauce. Stir in half the Parmesan.

Serve with the remaining Parmesan.

'Pancetta is the cured belly of pork either salted and dried (stesa) or smoked (affumicata). Pancetta stesa is sometimes cured with herbs such as rosemary and/or black pepper. Pancetta affumicata is usually leaner and should be cut finer as it can be tough.

We try to use a fatty stesa in this recipe, slowly cooked to release its delicious juices.

When choosing pancetta, look for even layers of fat and meat and a sweet perfume – a porky smell indicates lack of ageing and will affect the flavour of the sauce.'

Rigatoni, tomato, beef, red wine

Rigatoni	320g
Beef fillet	200g
Garlic cloves	4
Parmesan	50g
Unsalted butter	100g
Tin tomatoes	600g
Chianti wine	350ml
Ground black pepper	1 tbs
Ex. v. olive oil	3 tbs

Trim the fillet and cut across into 5mm slices. Cut the slices into 1cm strips. Peel and slice the garlic. Grate the Parmesan.

Heat the butter in a thick-bottomed pan, add the garlic and fry gently until brown. Add the tomatoes and season. Cook over a high heat for 5 minutes, stirring to break up the tomatoes, then add half the red wine. Continue to cook quite fast, adding more wine as the sauce reduces. Cook for a total of 15 minutes, using up all the wine, then stir in the pepper.

Heat the olive oil in a frying pan until very hot. Add the beef pieces and fry very briefly, just to brown each piece on each side. Stir the beef into the sauce with any juices from the pan.

Cook the rigatoni in boiling salted water until al dente. Drain and add to the sauce.

Serve with the Parmesan.

'Red wine is traditionally added to meat-based sauces. Here the wine is reduced with the tomatoes before the beef is added. In sausage sauces from Tuscany the wine is cooked with the sausage to soften and sweeten the flavour. All'Amatriciana is the Roman sauce where red wine is added to the crisp onion and pancetta base used to flavour the tomato.'

5

Fish pasta

Linguine, sardine, saffron
Bucatini, sardine, salted anchovy
Orecchiette, scallop, rocket
Spaghetti, squid, zucchini
Taglierini, clam, fried zucchini
Ditaloni, mussels, white wine
Tagliatelle, langoustine, ricotta
Orecchiette, clam, broccoli
Tagliatelle, brown shrimp, pea
Linguine, clam, white asparagus
Spaghetti, roasted red mullet
Tagliatelle, zucchini, mullet
Linguine, crab

Linguine, sardine, saffron

Linguine	320g
Sardines	12
Garlic cloves	2
Flat-leaf parsley leaves	2 tbs
Dried chillies	2
Saffron threads	½ tsp
Ex. v. olive oil	
Pine nuts	50g
Raisins	50g
Lemon	1

Fillet the sardines. Peel and finely slice the garlic. Chop the parsley and crumble the chillies. Sprinkle the saffron threads over 3 tbs hot water and let stand for 20 minutes. Soak the raisins in warm water for 20 minutes. Cut the lemon in quarters.

Heat 3 tbs olive oil in a heavy-bottomed pan and fry the garlic and parsley. Add the sardine fillets in one layer and fry gently for 2 minutes or until cooked through, spooning over the garlic and parsley. Season.

In a separate frying pan, brown the pine nuts.

Cook the linguine in boiling salted water until al dente, then drain and return to the pot. Drain the raisins and add to the pasta with the saffron. Toss to combine. Add the sardines and juices from the pan and check the seasoning. Scatter over the pine nuts.

Serve drizzled with olive oil and lemon.

'Pasta with sardines is one of the classic dishes from Sicily. As in any beloved regional recipe, the ingredients vary from cook to cook. This version includes the traditional pine nuts and raisins, but has the addition of saffron. Buy the threads not the powder: the colour should be deep orange.'

Fish pasta

Bucatini, sardine, salted anchovy

Bucatini	320g
Sardines	12
Red onion	1
Garlic cloves	2
Salted anchovies	4
Fennel seeds	1 tbs
Dried chillies	2
Capers	50g
Ex. v. olive oil	
Tin tomatoes	400g
White wine	150ml

Fillet the sardines. Peel and finely slice the onion and garlic. Wash the anchovies free of salt, fillet then roughly chop. Grind the fennel seeds. Crumble the chilli. Rinse the capers.

Heat 1 tbs olive oil in a small thick-bottomed pan. Add half the garlic, and fry until golden, then add the tomato and salt. Simmer for 20 minutes.

Heat 2 tbs olive oil in a large flat thick-bottomed frying pan. Gently fry the onion until soft and beginning to colour. Add the anchovies, the remaining garlic, the fennel seeds and chilli, and cook together to melt the anchovy and soften the garlic.

Lay the sardine fillets in one layer over this mixture. Spoon over 3-4 tbs of the tomato sauce and season generously. Pour in the wine, sprinkle with the capers, then cover and cook for 3-4 minutes or until the sardines are cooked and the wine has combined with the sauce.

Cook the bucatini in boiling salted water until al dente. Drain and add to the sardines. Toss together in the pan over heat. Check for seasoning.

Serve with olive oil drizzled over.

Orecchiette, scallop, rocket

Orecchiette	320g
Large scallops	8
Rocket leaves	100g
Cherry tomatoes	500g
Garlic cloves	2
Fresh red chillies	2
Lemon	1
Ex. v. olive oil	

Cut the scallops into quarters. Wash, dry and chop the rocket. Cut the tomatoes in half, and squeeze out the seeds and juice. Peel and finely chop the garlic. Cut the chillies in half lengthways, scrape out the seeds and finely chop. Cut the lemon into 4 wedges.

Put the tomato pieces in a bowl, and add the chilli, garlic and 2 tbs olive oil. Season generously and put aside.

Heat 1 tbs olive oil in a thick-bottomed frying pan, and add the scallops. Season and fry briefly until brown, then stir in the marinated tomatoes. Cook only briefly, just to combine.

Cook the orecchiette in boiling salted water until al dente, then drain and add to the pan. Stir in the rocket, and test for seasoning.

Serve drizzled with olive oil, with a squeeze of lemon.

Spaghetti, squid, zucchini

Spaghetti	320g
Squid	500g
Zucchini	400g
Garlic cloves	2
Dried chilli	1
Lemon	1
Ex. v. olive oil	
Marjoram leaves	2 tbs

Prepare the squid by pulling away the head and tentacles from the body. Cut off the tentacles and squeeze out the beak. Open the body out into a flat piece and scrape away the soft interior pulp. Finely slice the body. Separate the tentacles. Wash and pat dry.

Wash and grate the zucchini at an angle on the large side of a cheese grater. Sprinkle with salt and put in a colander to drain for 15 minutes. Wash off the salt and pat dry.

Peel and finely slice the garlic. Crumble the chilli. Grate the rind of the lemon finely, and then squeeze the juice.

Heat a large thick-bottomed frying pan, add 3 tbs olive oil and when smoking hot, add the squid. Stir briefly, then add salt, pepper and chilli, followed by the zucchini and garlic. Stir-fry just to brown the squid and soften the zucchini. Add the lemon juice and zest and the marjoram, and stir. Remove from the heat.

Cook the spaghetti in boiling salted water, then drain and add to the squid mixture. Toss.

Serve drizzled with olive oil.

Fish pasta

Taglierini, clam, fried zucchini

Taglierini	320g
Clams	1 kg
Zucchini	500g
Garlic clove	1
Flat-leaf parsley leaves	1 tbs
Dried chilli	1
Ex. v. olive oil	
White wine	250ml
Unsalted butter	30g

Wash the clams. Trim the ends of the zucchini and slice as finely as possible into discs. Peel and finely chop the garlic. Finely chop the parsley. Crumble the chilli.

In a thick-bottomed pan heat 1 tbs olive oil. Fry the garlic and chilli for a minute, then add the clams and white wine. Cover and cook over a high heat until the clams open, about 3 minutes. Drain, reserving the liquid. Take the clams out of the shells, and discard the shells.

Return the clam liquid to the pan and boil to reduce by half. Lower the heat and stir in the butter.

Heat 5 tbsp olive oil in a heavy-bottomed frying pan and cook the zucchini in one layer until lightly brown on both sides. Drain on kitchen paper. Season.

Cook the taglierini in boiling salted water until al dente. Drain and add to the sauce, along with the clams. Toss well.

Serve with the zucchini on top.

Ditaloni, mussels, white wine

Ditaloni	320g
Mussels	1kg
Garlic cloves	2
Flat-leaf parsley leaves	4 tbs
Unsalted butter	200g
Ex. v. olive oil	1 tbs
White wine	120ml
Double cream	150ml

Scrub the mussels. Peel and finely chop the garlic. Finely chop the parsley.

Heat half the butter with the oil, then add the garlic and mussels. Pour in the wine, season, cover and cook over a high heat until the mussels open. Drain the mussels, keeping the cooking liquid. Remove the mussels from the shells, and discard the shells and any that haven't opened.

Heat the remaining butter in a pan, and add the mussel juices and the cream. Cook gently to reduce to a rich, creamy consistency. Then add the mussels and parsley.

Cook the ditaloni in boiling salted water until al dente, then drain and add to the sauce. Toss together over a low heat and serve.

'Ditaloni is a small tubular pasta. Cavatelle or short penne can be used as an alternative. Buy small mussels so they are the same size as the pasta.'

Fish pasta

Tagliatelle, langoustine, ricotta

Tagliatelle	320g
Langoustines	2kg
Lemons	2
Dried chilli	1
Ricotta	300g
Ex. v. olive oil	
Basil leaves	3 tbs

Grate the zest of 1 of the lemons, and squeeze the juice. Cut the other lemon into wedges. Crumble the chilli.

Lightly beat the ricotta, add half the lemon juice and all the zest, and then stir in the olive oil. Season generously.

Cook the langoustines in boiling salted water for 2 minutes, then drain and peel off the shell. Cut each in half lengthways. Season whilst warm, and drizzle with a little oil and lemon juice.

Cook the tagliatelle in boiling salted water until al dente, then drain and stir into the ricotta. Add the langoustines and the basil torn into pieces.

Serve with pieces of lemon.

'We first encountered this idea of combining fish and ricotta at the famous restaurant Romano in Viareggio. In this recipe, the light creaminess of the ricotta with the freshly boiled langoustines makes a unique summer pasta.'

Orecchiette, clam, broccoli

Orecchiette	320g
Clams	1kg
Broccoli	300g
Garlic cloves	3
Fresh red chilli	1
Flat-leaf parsley leaves	1 tbs
Dried chilli	1
Ex. v. olive oil	
Anchovy fillets	3
White wine	150ml

Wash the clams. Cut the spears from the broccoli head. Discard the big stalks. Cut each spear in two lengthways. Peel and finely chop the garlic. Deseed and chop the fresh chilli and chop the parsley. Crumble the dried chilli.

Cook the broccoli spears in boiling salted water until very tender.

Heat 2 tbs olive oil in a thick-bottomed pan. Add half the garlic and fry until soft, and then add the anchovies and dried chilli. Stir to melt the anchovies, then add the broccoli and cook for 10 minutes until it breaks up and becomes a sauce.

Heat 2 tbs olive oil in a large pan. Add the fresh chilli, remaining garlic and parsley, and fry until just brown. Add the clams and wine, cover and cook over a high heat until the clams open, about 3 minutes. Drain, reserving the liquid.

Remove the clams from their shells, and add to the broccoli with enough of their cooking liquid to make the sauce thinner.

Cook the orecchiette in boiling salted water until al dente. Drain and add to the sauce, stirring well to combine, and adding more liquid as necessary.

Serve with olive oil.

Tagliatelle, brown shrimp, pea

Tagliatelle	320g
Brown shrimps	300g
Frozen peas	500g
Garlic cloves	2
Mint leaves	2 tbs
Lemon	1
Unsalted butter	150g

Peel and finely chop the garlic. Coarsely chop the mint. Squeeze the lemon.

Melt half the butter in a thick-bottomed pan and add the garlic. Fry until soft, then add the shrimps. Stir to combine, then season, and add half the lemon juice.

Cook the peas until tender in boiling salted water. Drain and add to the shrimps.

Cook the tagliatelle in boiling salted water until al dente. Drain and add to the shrimps and peas. Add the mint and the remaining butter and lemon juice, toss well, check the seasoning, and serve.

'We use the small, cold water, pre-peeled brown shrimps – the same as those found in traditional English potted shrimp. You can still collect brown shrimps at low tide around the sandy coasts and estuaries of the UK.'

Linguine, clam, white asparagus

Linguine	320g
Clams	1kg
White asparagus	500g
Cinnamon stick	3cm
Unsalted butter	200g
White wine	110ml
Parmesan	50g

Wash the clams. Snap off the tough ends of the asparagus, peel the stalks, then cut each stalk lengthways into fine ribbons. Break up the cinnamon. Grate the Parmesan.

Heat half the butter gently in a large heavy-bottomed pan. Add the cinnamon, clams and wine, and season. Cover and cook over a high heat to open the clams, about 3 minutes. Drain, reserving the liquid. Remove half of the clam shells. Return the clams to the liquid.

Cook the linguine in boiling salted water for 6 minutes, then add the asparagus and cook together until the pasta is al dente. Drain and return to the pan. Add the remaining butter and the clams and their juices. Check for seasoning.

Serve with Parmesan.

'The combination of white asparagus, butter and cinnamon as a pasta sauce for clams was introduced to us in Verona's famous fish restaurant Osteria all'Oste Scuro.'

Spaghetti, roasted red mullet

Spaghetti	320g
Red mullet	2 x 500g
Small black olives	100g
Dried chillies	2
Cherry tomatoes	400g
Ex. v. olive oil	
Thyme leaves	1 tbs

Preheat the oven to 200°C/Gas 6.

Ask your fishmonger to fillet the mullet. Stone the olives. Crumble the chilli.

Toss the cherry-vine tomatoes with a little olive oil. Season and put in a baking tin in one layer. Prick each with a fork. Roast in the preheated oven for 20 minutes.

Place the mullet fillets in one layer in a shallow baking dish, and sprinkle with thyme and chilli, season. Drizzle with olive oil and roast in the preheated oven for 5 minutes.

Cook the spaghetti in boiling salted water until al dente. Drain and return to the pan.

Add the olives and tomatoes to the pasta, with 1 tbs olive oil and season. Add the mullet and toss gently. Serve.

'Mullet has a strong flavour and firm flesh so that it stays intact when tossed together with the olives, tomatoes and spaghetti. It is the most perishable of fish and should be eaten on the day it is bought.'

Fish pasta

Tagliatelle, zucchini, mullet

Egg tagliatelle	320g
Red mullet	4 x 350g
Zucchini	500g
Garlic cloves	3
Plum tomatoes	6
Lemons	2
Basil leaves	3 tbs
Ex. v. olive oil	

Ask the fishmonger to fillet the mullet. Slice the fillets across into 1cm pieces. Wash and grate the zucchini at an angle on the coarse side of the grater. Put in a colander and scatter over 1 tbs sea salt. Leave for 15 minutes, then squeeze dry. Peel and cut the garlic into fine slivers. Skin the tomatoes (see page 66), and roughly chop. Squeeze the juice of 1 lemon; quarter the other.

Heat 1 tsp oil in a thick-bottomed pan, add the garlic and brown lightly. Add the tomatoes, half the basil, and season with sea salt. Cook for 15 minutes.

Cook the tagliatelle with the zucchini in boiling salted water until al dente. Drain.

Add the mullet pieces to the hot tomato sauce, and pour over the lemon juice. Season the fish, then stir to combine. Mix the pasta and zucchini into the sauce, and add the remaining basil leaves.

Serve with the lemon pieces and a drizzle of olive oil.

Linguine, crab

Linguine	320g
Crabmeat	400g
Fennel bulb	1
Garlic clove	1
Fennel seeds	1 tbs
Dried chillies	2
Lemon	1
Ex. v. olive oil	

Remove the tough outer part and stalk of the fennel. Slice the bulb as finely as you can across the grain. Keep any of the green tops. Peel and finely chop the garlic. Crush the fennel seeds and crumble the chilli. Grate the zest of the lemon, and squeeze the juice.

Heat 2 tbs oil in a thick-bottomed pan, add the garlic, fennel seeds and chilli, and cook to soften. Add the crab, lemon juice and zest, and season. Stir through, just to heat up the crab.

Cook the linguine in boiling salted water for 5 minutes, then add the fennel slices, and cook together until al dente. Drain the pasta, keeping a little of the water, and add to the crab mixture. Stir thoroughly to combine, adding a little of the reserved water to loosen the sauce if necessary.

Serve with olive oil.

'If cooking crab yourself, buy them live and choose one or two large crabs which will be easier to pick the meat out from than many small ones. Cock crabs (males) have larger claws and a higher proportion of white meat.

Spider crabs are very sweet and good for this recipe, though it takes longer to pick out the meat than the common crab as the meat-to-shell ratio is less.'

Fish pasta

6

Really easy soups

Asparagus, prosciutto

Asparagus	500g
Prosciutto	150g
Red onion	1
Medium potatoes	2
Spinach	150g
Stock cubes	2
Flat-leaf parsley leaves	2 tbs
Ex. v. olive oil	

Remove the tough ends from the asparagus, and cut the remaining stems into 2-3cm lengths. Keep the tips to one side. Slice the prosciutto into ribbons. Peel and chop the onion. Peel the potatoes and cut into 1cm cubes. Wash the spinach. Dissolve the stock cubes in 700ml boiling water. Chop the parsley.

Heat 2 tbs oil in a thick-bottomed pan, add the onion and soften for 5 minutes, then add the prosciutto, potato, parsley and asparagus stems. Season and cook for 5 minutes, stirring, then add the stock and simmer until the potato and asparagus are tender, about 15 minutes. Add the spinach and the asparagus tips and cook for a further 3 minutes. Remove from the heat and blend the soup to a rough purée, keeping a few of the tips aside.

Heat 3 tbs olive oil and fry the reserved tips just for a few seconds. Serve the soup with the tips and the oil they were fried in drizzled over each bowl.

Tomato, chickpea, sage

Dried chickpeas	200g
Bicarbonate of soda	1 tsp
Plain flour	1 tsp
Celery stalks	2
Tin tomatoes	400g
Garlic cloves	3
Sage leaves	8
Ex. v. olive oil	
Ditaloni	100g

Soak the chickpeas overnight with the bicarbonate and flour. Drain, and rinse. Put the chickpeas into a thick-bottomed saucepan, cover with water, add the celery. Bring to the boil, skim and simmer for 35-40 minutes until soft, season. Drain the tomatoes of their juices, and roughly chop. Peel the garlic and finely slice. Chop the sage.

Heat 2 tbs olive oil in a thick-bottomed pan and fry the garlic and sage together for 2-3 minutes. Add the chickpeas, the tomatoes, salt and pepper, and stir. Bring to a simmer, then cook for 20 minutes.

Cook the pasta in boiling salted water until al dente, then drain. Toss with olive oil and seasoning.

In a food processor, pulse-chop the chickpea mixture. It should be very thick.

Stir the pasta into the soup, and serve with olive oil stirred into each portion.

'This soup is from the Capezzana wine and olive oil estate in Carmignano near Florence. They make it there at the beginning of November to show off their newly pressed, beautifully spicy and thick, green olive oil.'

Bread, tomato, basil, cucumber

Tomatoes	4
Cucumber	1
Garlic clove	1
Fresh red chillies	2
Ciabatta slices	4
Red wine vinegar	4 tbs
Ex. v. olive oil	
Basil leaves	4 tbs

Skin the tomatoes (see page 66), cut in half, and squeeze out the seeds. Chop the flesh to a pulp and put in a bowl. Peel the cucumber, cut in half and half again lengthways, then cut out the seeds. Chop the flesh finely. Peel and finely chop the garlic with a tsp of sea salt. Cut the chillies in half lengthways, scrape out the seeds, and finely chop. Add everything to the tomatoes.

Soak the ciabatta slices in a little cold water so they are thoroughly moist. Sprinkle with the vinegar, and leave for 10 minutes.

Squeeze out the bread and chop finely. Stir into the tomato mixture. Add black pepper and 3 tbs of olive oil and mix thoroughly.

Tear the basil into small pieces and stir into the soup. Serve with more olive oil.

'The Tuscan tradition of adding bread to soups is exemplified by the Florentine soup, Pappa Pomodoro. We have four different recipes in our previous books. This is a light, uncooked version and is very easy to make.'

Borlotti bean, pappardelle

Fresh borlotti beans	1kg
Potatoes	200g
Parsley leaves	1 tbs
Sage leaves	1 tbs
Rosemary leaves	8
Garlic cloves	2
Pancetta slices	100g
Ex. v. olive oil	
Pappardelle	50g

Pod the borlotti beans. Peel the potatoes and cut into 3mm cubes. Chop the parsley, sage and rosemary finely. Peel and finely chop the garlic. Cut the pancetta into fine matchsticks.

In a thick-bottomed saucepan heat 2 tbs of olive oil, add the chopped herbs and garlic and fry gently for 5 minutes. Add the pancetta, cook until soft, then stir in the potato and beans. Add enough hot water to cover, bring to the boil and cook until the beans are soft, about half an hour. Season.

Put the mixture into a food processor and blend until thick. Return to the saucepan.

Just before serving, cook the pappardelle in boiling salted water until al dente. Drain and add to the soup.

Serve with olive oil.

'Almost every region in Italy has versions of bean soup. This version from Milan has pappardelle, a fresh, wide ribbon egg pasta. In Venice, it is made with small, dried tubular pasta.'

Really easy soups

Chickpea, pork

Dried chickpeas	200g
Bicarbonate of soda	1 tsp
Pork belly	500g
Celery head	1
Medium potatoes	2
Carrot	1
Bay leaf	1
Ex. v. olive oil	

Soak the dried chickpeas overnight, adding the bicarbonate of soda to the water.

Cut the pork belly into 5cm pieces. Wash the celery and discard the outer stalks; cut the pale heart into quarters. Peel the potatoes and cut into 1cm cubes. Wash and halve the carrot.

Drain the chickpeas and rinse in cold water. Put in a thick-bottomed saucepan with the pork, vegetables and bay leaf. Just cover with water and bring to the boil, skimming if necessary. Turn down the heat, and simmer gently for 2 hours or until the pork is soft.

Break up the cooked vegetables into the chickpea liquid with a fork, and season generously.

Serve with a drizzle of olive oil.

'This is a very basic soup which we ate in Masuelli, a restaurant in Milan. The broth is simply the cooking water of the combined ingredients.'

Savoy cabbage, ricotta crostini

Savoy cabbage	½
Garlic clove	1
Parmesan	50g
Ricotta	100g
Ex. v. olive oil	
Ciabatta slices	4
Chicken stock cubes	3

Remove the tough outer leaves of the cabbage and core. Slice the cabbage and wash thoroughly. Peel the garlic, and grate the Parmesan. Dissolve the stock cubes in a litre of boiling water.

Mix the ricotta with salt and pepper and 1 tbs olive oil and season.

Bring the stock to the boil, add the cabbage, and cook until very tender.

Grill the crostini and lightly rub with garlic. Drizzle lightly with olive oil and put a spoonful of ricotta on top, pressing gently into the surface.

Place a crostini in each soup bowl. Spoon over the cabbage, then ladle in the stock.

Drizzle olive oil over and serve sprinkled with Parmesan.

'Good quality stock cubes are an easy alternative to homemade broth. Italians would make their own broth with a boiling fowl, celery, carrots, parsley and onion, boiled for 2-2½ hours. Traditionally, clear soups include either pasta or crostini to make the soup more of a meal.'

Pea, zucchini

Zucchini	500g
Garlic cloves	2
Parmesan	50g
Stock cubes	2
Ex. v. olive oil	
Podded fresh peas	500g
Basil leaves	3 tbs

Trim the ends of the zucchini, cut them in half lengthways, and then into 1cm pieces. Peel and chop the garlic. Grate the Parmesan. Dissolve the stock cubes in 700ml boiling water.

In a thick-bottomed saucepan, heat 2 tbs of the olive oil and fry the garlic until soft. Add the zucchini and cook, stirring until soft. Add half the peas, stir and then add half the stock. Cook until the peas are tender. Put into a food processor and pulse-chop to a coarse purée.

Bring the remaining peas to the boil in the remaining stock, and cook for 5 minutes. Scoop out the peas with a slotted spoon, and stir into the soup, adding a little of the stock if the soup is too thick.

Serve with torn basil leaves and grated Parmesan.

'Italian soups are distinctly thick – in this recipe we pulse-chop the cooked vegetables in a food processor and add more peas at the end. Frozen petit pois work just as well.'

Mushroom, barley

Dried porcini	35g
Barley	75g
Field mushrooms	350g
Medium potatoes	200g
Red onion	1
Garlic cloves	2
Parsley leaves	1 tbs
Sage leaves	1 tbs
Stock cubes	2
Bay leaf	1
Ex. v. olive oil	
Tin tomatoes	200g

Soak the porcini in 300ml boiling water for 10 minutes. Cook the barley in plenty of water, for 1 hour or until soft, and drain.

Chop the mushrooms coarsely, and peel and cut the potatoes into 3mm cubes. Peel and finely chop the onion and garlic, and finely chop the parsley and sage.

Drain the porcini, reserving the liquid and strain through muslin. Rinse the porcini and chop. Dissolve the stock cubes in 700ml boiling water and add the bay leaf.

In a heavy-bottomed saucepan heat 3 tbs olive oil. Add half the garlic, all the onion and herbs, and cook until soft. Add the potato, stirring until lightly browned. Stir in the tomatoes and add the stock and the porcini liquid. Simmer until the vegetables are very soft.

Heat 2 tbs olive oil in a frying pan, and fry the remaining garlic and the porcini until soft. Add the mushrooms, season, and cook for a further 10 minutes until dark.

Mix the barley and mushrooms into the soup. Serve with a drizzle of olive oil.

Pumpkin, mascarpone

Pumpkin	800g
Medium potatoes	· 3
Garlic cloves	3
Fennel seeds	1 tsp
Plum tomatoes	250g
Stock cubes	2
Parmesan	50g
Mascarpone	150g
Ex. v. olive oil	

Peel and deseed the pumpkin, and cut into 2cm cubes. Peel the potatoes, and cut into 2cm cubes. Peel the garlic, and grind the fennel seeds. Blanch and skin the tomatoes (see page 66). Dissolve the stock cubes in 500ml boiling water. Grate the Parmesan.

Put the potato, tomato, pumpkin and garlic cloves into a saucepan and just cover with the stock. Season, and add the fennel seeds. Simmer for 30 minutes, or until the vegetables are tender.

Mash the soup with a potato masher – it should be thick and creamy.

Serve with spoonfuls of mascarpone, olive oil and Parmesan.

'Pumpkins taste better when really ripe; the flesh should be close-textured and deep orange, the seeds plump. Peanut squash or butternut squash can be used instead, and tinned tomatoes, drained of excess juice, can replace the fresh tomatoes.'

Rice, chestnut

Chestnuts	500g
Tin borlotti beans	400g
Pancetta slices	100g
Rosemary sprig	1
Stock cube	1
Parmesan	75g
Unsalted butter	25g
Risotto rice	4 tbs
Milk	200ml

To remove the skins, make a shallow cut in each chestnut and place in a saucepan. Cover with water and boil for 15 minutes. Peel off the skins while the chestnuts are still hot. Roughly chop.

Drain and rinse the borlotti beans. Cut the pancetta into matchsticks. Finely chop the rosemary. Dissolve the stock cube in 500ml boiling water. Grate the Parmesan.

Heat the butter gently in a thick-bottomed saucepan, add the pancetta and rosemary and cook for 10 minutes to blend the flavours. Add the chestnuts, stir to coat them with butter, and cook for a few minutes. Add the rice, stirring it into the mixture, then slowly add the stock. As the rice begins to plump up, absorbing the stock, add the milk and cook for a further 20 minutes or until both the rice and chestnuts are soft.

Stir in the borlotti beans and more milk if too thick. Season, and serve with Parmesan.

'Substitute frozen chestnuts for fresh to save time. Tinned chestnuts are also good. You would need 2 x 400g tins for this recipe.'

Broccoli, red wine

Sprouting broccoli	**750g**
Garlic clove	**1**
Lambrusco red wine	**750ml**
Ex. v. olive oil	

Cut the spears from the broccoli heads. Discard the big stalks. Remove the bigger and tougher leaves. Cut each spear of broccoli in two. Peel and cut the garlic in half.

Put the broccoli and garlic into a medium thick-bottomed saucepan, then add enough of the wine to half cover the broccoli. Add a similar quantity of water to completely cover the broccoli. Season, cover, and simmer for 20 minutes.

Serve with a drizzle of olive oil.

'La Latteria is a tiny, family-run restaurant situated in an old dairy in the market in Milan, with just a few shared tables and wonderful, simple, original food. This seasonal soup using sprouting broccoli and young, local red wine such as Lambrusco is surprisingly delicious. Choose leafy purple sprouting broccoli and include the small leaves in the soup.'

7

Fish with...

Baked bass in the bag, fennel
Sea bass baked in sea salt
Poached turbot, salsa verde
Sea bass, potato, tomato
Langoustine, sea salt, olive oil
Grilled red mullet, crostini
Raw tuna, bruschetta
Fried scallop, borlotti
Crab, chilli, fennel

Baked bass in the bag, fennel

Sea bass	1 x 2kg
Fennel bulbs	2
Lemons	2
Dried chillies	2
Unsalted butter	200g
Extra dry vermouth	150ml

Ask your fishmonger to scale and fillet the fish. Divide each fillet into 2 to make 4 portions.

Preheat the oven to 200°C/Gas 6.

Remove the tough outer stalks and leaves of the fennel and slice lengthways, keeping the green tops. Finely grate the peel and squeeze the juice of 1 lemon; cut the second lemon into quarters. Crumble the chillies. Soften half of the butter.

Cook the fennel in boiling salted water for 4 minutes, drain and cool.

To make the bags, cut foil into 4 x 50cm lengths. Fold over to make 25cm squares. Smear each generously with soft butter, and season with salt and pepper. Place a piece of fish on the top half of the buttered foil, and cover with a few slices of fennel. Scatter with dried chilli, lemon zest and a few bits of fennel herb. Place a knob of butter on the fish. Bring the foil over the fish, and fold to seal each side, leaving the top open. Pour a little vermouth and lemon juice into each, then seal.

Place the bags on a tray and into the preheated oven. Bake for 15 minutes or until the bags inflate. Split open each bag, and serve.

Fish with...

Sea bass baked in sea salt

Sea bass	1 x 2kg
Lemons	2
Coarse sea salt	3kg
Rosemary sprigs	2
Ex. v. olive oil	

Ask your fishmonger to gut and remove the gills of the fish, but not to scale it. Cut the lemons into wedges.

Preheat the oven to 200°C/Gas 6.

Place the salt in a large bowl and add 250ml water. Stir to stiffen the salt to damp-sand consistency. Season the fish generously inside the cavity, and add the rosemary.

Using a large flat frying pan or a baking tray, cover the base with a thick layer of salt. Place the fish on top then pack the remaining salt over the fish, making sure you cover it evenly, see photograph on previous page.

Bake in the preheated oven for 15-20 minutes. To test, pierce the salt with a skewer and into the fish to the backbone, where the fish is thickest. Touch the end of the skewer: if it is hot, the fish is cooked.

Remove the fish from the oven to cool slightly. Break off the now hard salt crust from the top. Lift the fish off the salt base, then remove the skin from the top side. Fillet the fish to serve.

Place the fish on a plate, and serve with lemon wedges and a very good quality olive oil.

'Use a coarse-grained sea salt such as Costa, not Maldon salt, for this recipe.'

Fish with...

Poached turbot, salsa verde

Salsa verde

Flat-leaf parsley leaves	2 tbs
Mint leaves	1 tbs
Ex. v. olive oil	
Garlic clove	1
Capers	1 tbs
Anchovy fillets	3
Dijon mustard	1 tbs
Red wine vinegar	1 tbs
Turbot tranches	4
Fennel seeds	1 tbs
Garlic bulb	½
Parsley stalks	4
Black peppercorns	2 tbs
White wine	350ml

For the salsa verde, chop the parsley and mint, put into a bowl and cover with olive oil. Peel the garlic and chop with the capers and anchovies. Add to the herbs and mix. Stir in the mustard and vinegar, season and add more olive oil to loosen the sauce.

In a saucepan wide enough to fit the turbot pieces in one layer, add all the ingredients except for the fish. Add 1.5l of water and boil for 30 minutes.

Reduce to a simmer and add the fish. The fish should be covered by the liquid – top up with hot water if necessary. Poach for 10 minutes, then remove from the heat, and drain.

Serve hot or at room temperature, with the salsa verde.

'The flavour of the broth should be delicate and fresh. Choose a light dry white wine such as Pinot Bianco.'

Sea bass, potato, tomato

Sea bass fillets	4
Waxy potatoes	500g
Cherry tomatoes	250g
Rosemary sprigs	4
Ex. v. olive oil	
Anchovy fillets	8
White wine	450ml

Preheat the oven to 200°C/Gas 6.

Peel the potatoes. Cut the tomatoes in half and squeeze out the seeds and juice. Wash the rosemary sprigs.

Cook the potatoes in boiling salted water until cooked but still firm, then drain and cool. Cut the potatoes into 5mm thick slices.

Drizzle a baking tray with olive oil, and cover with the potatoes and tomato halves. Place the rosemary on top and season. Place the bass fillets on top and put 2 anchovies on each fillet with some black pepper, drizzle with olive oil.

Place in the preheated oven and bake for 6 minutes. Add the wine, return to the oven, and bake for a further 6 minutes.

Serve each portion with juices from the pan spooned over.

'Choose a thin-skinned yellow, waxy potato that will not break up when cooked a second time. Varieties to look for are Roseval, Ratte, Linska and Spunta.'

Langoustine, sea salt, olive oil

Langoustines	16
Parsley stalks	8
Bay leaves	2
Lemons	4
Marjoram leaves	2 tbs
Sea salt	
Black peppercorns	1 tbs
Ex. v. olive oil	

Wash the parsley stalks and bay leaves. Cut the lemons in half. Wash the marjoram and shake dry.

Bring a large pan of water to the boil. Add the parsley, bay leaves, 1 tbs of sea salt, peppercorns, and return to the boil. Add the langoustines, pushing them down so they are submerged. Cover and cook until the langoustines are firm, about 3-5 minutes according to size. Drain.

Cover a plate with a thin layer of sea salt. Lay the langoustines on top. Drizzle with olive oil and sprinkle with marjoram. Serve with lemon.

'We found this way of serving fresh, locally caught langoustines in Vernazza, a small village on the Ligurian coast. Perfect with just sea salt, fresh marjoram and olive oil.'

Grilled red mullet, crostini

Red mullet	4 x 500g
Salted anchovies	4
Rosemary leaves	1 tbs
Lemons	4
Small black olives	100g
Dried chilli	1
Thyme leaves	2 tbs
Ex. v. olive oil	
Ciabatta loaf	1
Garlic cloves	2

Prepare the anchovies (see page 42), and finely chop. Wash the rosemary. Squeeze the juice of 1 lemon; cut the others into quarters. Stone the olives, and crumble the chilli. Peel the garlic.

Put the anchovies in a bowl and mix with the lemon juice. Finely chop the rosemary and add to the anchovies, season with black pepper. Add 2 tbs olive oil and mix well.

Pulse-chop the olives in a food processor. Put in a bowl, and add the crumbled chilli, thyme leaves and enough olive oil to make a rough paste.

Season the mullet on all sides, brush with olive oil and grill, about 5 minutes on each side.

Cut the ciabatta into slices, grill on both sides, rub with garlic and drizzle with olive oil.

Put each mullet on a plate with the crostini, spread half with anchovy and half with olives. Serve with lemon.

Fish with...

Raw tuna, bruschetta

Tuna	500g
Lemon	1
Dried chillies	2
Sourdough loaf	¼
Ex. v. olive oil	
Sea salt	

Slice the tuna across the grain into thin slices 5mm thick. Halve the lemon, and crumble the chillies.

Cut the bread into 4 thick slices. Toast the bread on both sides. Drizzle with olive oil.

Serve the raw tuna beside the toast, sprinkled with chilli, black pepper and sea salt.
Serve with lemon.

'Tuccino, a seaside fish restaurant just south of Bari in Puglia, is where we ate a variety of raw fish. It was June when we were there, the season for Blue Fin tuna from the Mediterranean. The fish was incredibly fresh, the bread was made without salt, and lemon was the only accompaniment.'

Fish with...

Fried scallop, borlotti

Scallops	16
Dried borlotti	250g
Fresh red chillies	3
Garlic cloves	2
Rocket leaves	100g
Lemons	4
Ex. v. olive oil	

Soak the borlotti beans overnight. Rinse, then put into a saucepan with 1 chilli and the garlic. Bring to the boil, skim and simmer for 45 minutes. Drain, season and add olive oil. Keep warm. Slice the remaining chillies diagonally into 5mm slices, leaving the seeds in. Wash and dry the rocket. Halve the lemons. For the dressing, squeeze the juice of 1 lemon and combine with 3 times the volume of olive oil, season.

Heat a thick-bottomed frying pan large enough to hold the scallops in one layer.

Season the scallops on both sides. When the pan is very hot, sear the scallops 30 seconds on each side and remove.

Reduce the heat. Add 1 tbs olive oil to the pan, add the chillies. Squeeze over the juice of 1 lemon and shake the pan for a minute.

Chop the rocket leaves and toss with the dressing. Add the borlotti beans and divide between 4 plates. Place the scallops, chilli and any sauce from the pan on top. Serve with lemon.

Fish with...

Crab, chilli, fennel

For 2	
Live crabs	2 x 800g
Garlic cloves	8
Fresh root ginger	70g
Fennel seeds	1 tbs
Fresh red chillies	4
Fennel herb	4 tbs
Lemons	3
Tomatoes	4
Ex. v. olive oil	4 tbs
White wine	200ml

Peel and finely slice the garlic and ginger. Crush the fennel seeds. Wash and slice the chillies diagonally into rings, letting some of the seeds fall out. Wash and chop the fennel. Squeeze the juice of 2 lemons. Cut the remaining lemon into quarters. Peel, deseed and roughly chop the tomatoes.

Cut each crab in half and half again. Use a hammer to roughly break the shell in the claws and thicker legs.

Heat the oil in a large thick-bottomed pan with a well-fitting lid. Add the crab, garlic, ginger, fennel seeds and chilli. Stir briefly, then add the tomatoes, wine and half the lemon juice. Season generously with salt and pepper, cover and cook for 10 minutes.

Add the fennel and the remaining lemon juice. Serve with the juices in a large bowl, with a lemon quarter.

'You have to buy small crabs, one per person, for this recipe. The difficult part is cutting them up live. Versions of this recipe can be found from China through India and into the Mediterranean.'

8

Birds with wine

Roast grouse, Chianti Classico
Roast quail, Cabernet Sauvignon
Roast pheasant, Chardonnay
Roast partridge, Vin Santo
Pot-roast guinea fowl, Marsala
Roast wild duck, Nebbiolo
Roast teal, Pinot Bianco
Roast duck, Valpolicella
Roast chicken, Vermentino
Slow-roast chicken, Vermouth
Roast chicken, Pinot Grigio

Roast grouse, Chianti Classico

Grouse	4
Plum tomatoes	8
Sourdough loaf	¼
Sage leaves	2 tbs
Thyme sprigs	8
Unsalted butter	200g
Chianti Classico	500ml

Preheat the oven to 220°C/Gas 7.

Skin the tomatoes, leaving them whole (see page 66), and season them with sea salt. Cut the bread in 4 thick slices.

Stuff each bird with a few sage leaves, thyme sprigs and a knob of butter. Generously season inside and out.

Heat an oven dish, and melt half the butter. Add the grouse, breast-side down. Roast the birds in the preheated oven for 5 minutes, then turn them over. Add half the wine and the tomatoes, and cook for a further 15 minutes. Baste with the juices from the pan, and place the bread into the pan, soaking up some of the juices. Roast for a further 5-10 minutes, depending on how rare you like your birds.

Remove the birds, the tomatoes and bruschettas from the pan. Add the remaining butter and wine and, over a high heat, reduce to a thickish sauce.

Serve each bird on a tomato bruschetta with the wine sauce poured over.

'Chianti Classico is produced in the heart of Tuscany. The ripe fruit, spicy character and rich tannins of this wine are perfect for grouse, the gamiest of game birds.'

Roast quail,
Cabernet Sauvignon

Organic quail	8
Garlic cloves	8
Dried chillies	2
Ex. v. olive oil	3 tbs
Rosemary sprigs	4
Cabernet Sauvignon	250ml
Tin tomatoes	400g

Season the quails inside and out. Peel the garlic, keeping the cloves whole. Crumble the chillies. Wash the rosemary.

Heat the olive oil in a large thick-bottomed saucepan. Brown the quails on all sides, then add the garlic cloves, the rosemary sprigs and chilli and fry together for a minute. Add half the wine and let it reduce, then add the tomatoes and season. Lower the heat and cook with the lid half on for 10 minutes. Add the remaining red wine, and cook for a further 10-15 minutes. The quails should be almost falling apart, and the sauce thick.

Serve two quails each with Wet polenta (see page 276).

'Cabernet Sauvignon's subtle blackcurrant flavour and big tannins combine well with the tomatoes in this recipe.'

Roast pheasant, Chardonnay

Pheasant	2
Garlic cloves	4
Savoy cabbage	1
Unsalted butter	50g
Ex. v. olive oil	2 tbs
Pancetta slices	10
Sage leaves	3 tbs
Chardonnay	350ml

Preheat the oven to 180°C/Gas 4.

Wipe the pheasants inside and out and trim off the fat. Peel and cut the garlic in half lengthways. Remove the tough outer leaves from the cabbage, cut in half, and cut out the core. Slice into 2cm-wide strips.

In a casserole, heat the butter and 1 tbs olive oil. Brown the birds well. Add the pancetta, half the garlic and the sage. Cook to soften, then add the wine and bring to the boil. Roast in the preheated oven for 30-40 minutes, depending on size. Baste with the wine from time to time.

Cook the cabbage in boiling salted water until tender, about 8 minutes, then drain well.

Heat the remaining olive oil in a large saucepan, add the remaining garlic and fry until soft. Add the cabbage, stir to combine, season. Remove the pheasant from the casserole. Stir the cabbage into the wine juices and serve with the pheasant.

'Chardonnay is our favourite white wine for roasting pheasant, bringing richness, floral aroma and ripe tropical fruit flavours to the dish.'

Roast partridge, Vin Santo

Partridge	4
Quince	2
Pancetta slices	8
Unsalted butter	150g
Vin Santo	500ml

Preheat the oven to 220°C/Gas 7.

Wipe the down from the quinces, cut in half and then in half again. Take out the core.

Season the birds inside and out. Place 2 slices pancetta over the breasts of each bird, and secure with string.

Heat an ovenproof dish, and melt half the butter. Add the quince pieces and the birds, breast-side down, and brown briefly over a high heat. Pour in half the Vin Santo, and roast in the preheated oven for 10 minutes. Turn the birds and the quince over to brown on the other side. Add the remaining Vin Santo and roast for a further 10 minutes.

Serve the birds and quince with the juices from the pan.

'The season for partridge coincides with the quince season throughout most of Europe. If you have trouble finding quinces, you could use cooking apples instead.

Vin Santo, Tuscany's famous sweet wine, adds wonderful apricot and orange flavours and a syrupy texture to the dish. Avoid the artificially fortified liquoroso versions.'

Pot-roast guinea fowl, Marsala

Guinea fowl	2
Garlic cloves	4
Chicken stock cube	1
Prosciutto slices	8
Unsalted butter	150g
Ex. v. olive oil	2 tbs
Sage leaves	2 tbs
Marsala (dry)	500ml
Double cream	250ml

Peel the garlic. Dissolve the chicken stock cube in 400ml of boiling water.

Season the guinea fowl inside and out. Lay 4 prosciutto slices over the breasts of each bird, and secure with string.

Heat half the butter and the olive oil in a medium thick-bottomed saucepan, or a casserole, and brown the guinea fowl on all sides. Add the garlic and sage, then cook for 40-50 minutes over a low heat, starting with the birds on one breast, then turning on to the other breast, then finally breast-side up. Add the Marsala and stock bit by bit during the cooking. There should never be more than 1cm of liquid in the pan during cooking.

When cooked, remove the birds from the pan. Add the cream to the juices and reduce to thicken. Season.

Carve the birds, pouring the sauce over.

'Marsala doesn't deteriorate after opening, so is a great standby in the kitchen. Like sherry, it can be dry or sweet.'

Roast wild duck, Nebbiolo

Wild duck	2
Tomato sauce	8 tbs
Prosciutto slices	6
Nebbiolo	500ml

Make the tomato sauce (see page 66). Tear the prosciutto into pieces.

Preheat the oven to 200°C/Gas 6.

Season the cavity of each bird. Mix the prosciutto with the tomato sauce, divide in half, and stuff each bird. Push the tail into the bird to seal the cavity.

Place the birds breast-side down in a roasting tray, and pour over half the wine. Roast for 20 minutes. Turn the birds over, pour in the rest of the wine, and roast for a further 20-30 minutes. The breast will be medium cooked. The legs will always be tougher on wild ducks. Longer cooking will give them a chance to become more tender, but the breast will then be well done.

Serve the birds with some of the tomato stuffing, which will have combined with the wine to make a thick sauce.

'We use a basic Nebbiolo for cooking. The aged, more expensive and grand examples of this wine, Barolo and Barbaresco, we reserve for drinking.'

Roast teal, Pinot Bianco

Teal	4
Garlic cloves	4
Lemon	½
Ex. v. olive oil	4 tbs
Thyme sprigs	6
Pinot Bianco	350ml
Rocket leaves	250g

Preheat the oven to 180°C/Gas 4.

Season the teal inside and out. Peel and cut the garlic in half lengthways. Squeeze the lemon.

In a casserole large enough to hold the 4 teal, heat 2 tbs olive oil and brown the teal on all sides. Add the garlic and thyme, and fry for a minute, then add the wine and seasoning. Bring to the boil, then roast in the preheated oven for about 30 minutes.

Remove from the oven and let rest for 10 minutes.

Combine the lemon juice and remaining olive oil, and season. Pour over the rocket leaves, and toss.

Serve the teal with the juices poured over, the rocket and borlotti beans (see page 277).

'Pinot Bianco's lean, mineral character and floral aromas are excellent with the more delicate flavours of this tiny wild duck.'

Birds with wine

Roast duck, Valpolicella

Large duck	1
Purple figs	16
Valpolicella	350ml
Unsalted butter	200g

Place the figs in a bowl and pour in the wine, pushing the figs down so they are immersed. Cover and leave to marinate for 1 hour.

Preheat the oven to 180°C/Gas 4.

Remove the fat from the cavity of the duck, and season the inside generously. Put 50g butter and 8 of the figs inside the cavity. Smear the remaining butter over the breasts.

Put the duck in a roasting tray, breast-side down, and roast for 45 minutes. Drain off the fat. Turn over, add the remaining figs and the wine, and roast for a further hour, basting from time to time.

Skim off any excess fat and serve with the figs and juices from the pan.

'Made from the Corvina grape, Valpolicella is meant to be enjoyed young. Its bitter cherry and almond flavours and refreshing acidity are a perfect balance to the fat-rich duck.'

Birds with wine

Roast chicken, Vermentino

Organic chicken	2kg
Waxy potatoes	1kg
Dried porcini	75g
Garlic cloves	2
Rosemary sprig	1
Ex. v. olive oil	
Vermentino	250ml

Ask the butcher to cut up the chicken into 8 pieces. Wipe the pieces clean and trim off any fat.

Preheat the oven to 200°C/Gas 6.

Peel the potatoes and slice them in half lengthways and in half again. Soak the porcini in 400ml hot water for 10 minutes, drain, keeping the water. Rinse and roughly chop. Peel and finely slice the garlic. Wash and chop the rosemary.

Heat a medium frying pan with 1 tbs olive oil, add the garlic and lightly brown. Add the porcini, stir and cook for 2 minutes. Add a little of the liquid, stir, and gently simmer, adding more liquid to keep the mushrooms quite wet. Season.

Put the chicken in a roasting tray in one layer. Add the potatoes, the rosemary, the wine and 3 tbs olive oil. Stir in the porcini, season. Roast for 30 minutes. Turn the chicken over and continue cooking for 30 minutes. The chicken and potatoes should be light brown. Serve with the juices from the pan.

'Good Vermentino has a zippy, lemony acidity with peachy fruit and a hint of fresh herbs – great with potatoes and porcini.'

Birds with wine

Slow-roast chicken, Vermouth

Organic chicken	2kg
Garlic cloves	3
Sage leaves	2 tbs
Rosemary sprigs	2
Unsalted butter	150g
Extra dry Vermouth	100ml

Preheat the oven to 80°C/the very lowest gas.

Wipe the chicken clean and trim off all the excess fat.

Season the cavity. Peel the garlic, wash the rosemary and sage and stuff into the chicken.

Place the chicken upside down in a roasting tin just large enough to hold it. Add 200ml water. Cook for an hour, then turn on to the right side. Return to the oven and cook for another hour, then turn to the other side and cook for yet another hour.

Remove the chicken from the oven, raise the heat to 200°C/Gas 6. Rub the butter all over the skin, season well, and put the Vermouth in the pan.

Return to the oven, and cook for half an hour or until brown. Drain the fat and serve with the juices from the pan.

'Vermouth, both red and white, is made from wine flavoured with aromatic herb extracts and spices. We use extra dry white vermouth for this recipe which gives the chicken a herbal flavour.'

Birds with wine

Roast chicken, Pinot Grigio

Organic chicken	2kg
Garlic cloves	6
Rosemary sprigs	8
Lemon	1
Unsalted butter	220g
White wine	250ml

Preheat the oven to 180°C/Gas 4.

Wipe the chicken clean, and trim off excess fat. Peel and finely slice the garlic. Wash the rosemary, take the leaves off two sprigs. Halve the lemon.

Season the cavity, insert the garlic and rosemary leaves, with half the butter. Tuck a sprig of rosemary under each wing, and tie to secure. Rub the skin of the chicken with a half lemon and salt.

In a roasting pan melt the rest of the butter. Place the chicken on its side with the rest of the rosemary underneath. Put into the oven and roast for 20 minutes. Turn the bird over and roast on the other side for a further 20 minutes. Then put it breast-side down, and add half the wine and the other half lemon. Roast for a further 40 minutes.

Remove the chicken and rosemary from the pan, and skim off the excess fat. Over heat, add the remaining wine, cook for 5 minutes. Season, strain and pour over the chicken

'The fresh, light and appley character of this wine is a good complement to the strong flavour of rosemary.'

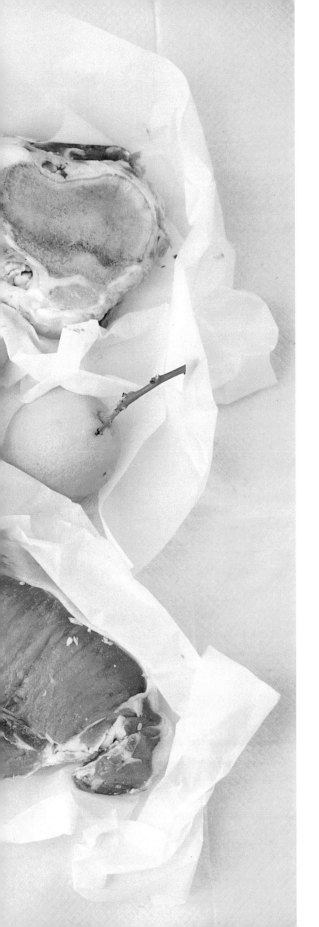

9

Roast meat

Whole leg of lamb, rosemary

Leg of lamb	1
Lemons	2
Garlic cloves	2
Small rosemary sprigs	2 tbs
Ex. v. olive oil	

Preheat the oven to 200°C/Gas 6.

Peel the lemons, and cut the rind into small pieces. Squeeze the juice. Peel and slice the garlic.

Cut small slits all over the leg, 1cm deep, and stuff a little of the garlic, rosemary and lemon inside each. Season well, and rub with olive oil.

Place the lamb in a roasting tin and roast for 30 minutes. Remove from the oven and pour over the lemon juice. Reduce the heat to 150°C/Gas 2, and roast for another hour, covered with foil.

Transfer to a board or serving plate, and leave to rest for 10-15 minutes. Tilt the roasting tin to remove as much fat as possible, then pour the juices over the lamb.

'New season's lamb is available from mid-April through to December from lambs which are born the same year. The flavour of grass-fed lamb develops, getting stronger throughout the year.

Look for pale pink flesh with a very thin coating of white fat. The weight of a short leg is usually between 2.5 and 3kg and a full leg with chump between 3 and 4kg.'

Roast meat

Boned leg of lamb

Leg of lamb	1
Rosemary sprigs	3
Garlic cloves	6
Anchovy fillets	10
Lemons	2
Ex. v. olive oil	

Ask the butcher to remove just the long leg bone, keeping the butterflied flesh attached to the shank bone.

Preheat the oven to 160ºC/Gas 3.

Wash the rosemary. Pull the leaves from the stalks, peel and crush the garlic, and chop the anchovies. Squeeze 1 of the lemons; cut the other in half.

Finely chop the rosemary with the garlic and 1 tbs sea salt. Add a little of the lemon juice to make a paste and spread on the inside of the leg. Scatter over the anchovies, and roll the leg up into a sausage. Tie with string, and season.

Place in a roasting tin and drizzle with olive oil and the rest of the lemon juice. Roast in the oven for 45 minutes with the lemon halves, then turn the meat over, squeeze the cooked lemons over the meat, and continue cooking for a further 1¼ hours.

Remove the lamb from the pan to a serving plate and cut off the string. Add 3 tbs hot water to the pan, deglaze, and pour this juice over thick-cut slices.

Roast meat

Pork shoulder, slow-cooked

Pork shoulder	2kg
Garlic cloves	6
Lemon	1
Unsalted butter	150g
Ex. v. olive oil	2 tbs
Sage leaves	2 tbs
White wine	250ml
Milk	250ml

Ask your butcher to bone out the piece of shoulder and remove the skin. (For 4 people, you would need a half small shoulder.)

Peel the garlic and cut each clove in half. Peel the rind from the lemon.

Season the piece of pork generously all over.

Heat half the butter with the olive oil in a medium thick-bottomed saucepan with a lid, just large enough to hold the pork. Brown the meat on all sides. Drain off excess oil, then add the remaining butter, the garlic, sage and lemon peel. Fry to colour the garlic, then add half the wine. Reduce the heat, half cover and very slowly simmer for 3 hours, adding more wine to keep a fraction of liquid in the pan at all times.

Start adding the milk after all the wine has evaporated. The milk should begin to curdle and thicken in the last half-hour. The pork will be cooked when you can break it up with a spoon.

'Choose your pork shoulder carefully. It should have a thick layer of fat beneath the skin. The fat renders down in the very slow cooking, keeping the meat moist and tender.'

Pork loin on the bone

Pork loin	1.5kg
Rosemary sprigs	2
Garlic cloves	4
Ex. v. olive oil	

Ask your butcher to cut the loin from the bone, keeping the rib bones intact, and to trim just the rib bones so that you have the bone and the meat in two separate pieces.

Preheat the oven to 180°C/Gas 4.

Wash the rosemary, pull the leaves from the stalk. Peel the garlic. Chop the rosemary and garlic together with 1 tbs sea salt. Rub the rosemary mixture all over the meat, then put it back on the bone in its original position. Tie with string to secure.

Place the loin in a roasting tin and drizzle with olive oil. Roast for 1½-2 hours, turning the meat over from time to time. Add 3 tbs water to loosen the juices, whilst roasting.

Remove string, cut loin into thick slices, and serve with the concentrated juices from the pan.

'Pork is the popular meat of Tuscany. This recipe is known as Arista di Maiale and is the traditional Florentine way to roast pork loin on the bone.'

Thick veal chop, lemon zest

Veal loin chops	**4 x 3cm thick**
Lemons	**2**
Ex. v. olive oil	
Thyme leaves	**2 tbs**
Unsalted butter	**150g**

Preheat the oven to 200°C/Gas 6.

Wash and finely grate the rind of the lemons. Season the chops and put in a bowl with 2 tbs of the olive oil, the lemon zest and thyme. Marinate for 20 minutes and remove onto kitchen paper.

In an ovenproof pan large enough to hold the chops in one layer, melt half the butter with 2tbs of olive oil. Seal the chops over a high heat to get a dark colour. Remove the chops from the pan, and discard the fat. Wipe the pan with kitchen paper.

Return the chops to the pan, and divide the remaining butter over both chops. Season well. Put into the preheated oven and roast for 15 minutes.

Squeeze over the lemon juice, and serve.

'Roasting a very thick chop, rather than grilling, helps keep the meat more succulent and juicy. It is important to seal the chop first over high heat. Serve with salsa verde (see page 131).'

Veal shin, butter, white wine

Veal shin	1
Garlic cloves	14
Ciabatta slices	4
Unsalted butter	100g
Thyme sprigs	3-4
White wine	200ml
Ex. v. olive oil	

Preheat the oven to 200ºC/Gas 6.

Season the meat generously. Peel the garlic.

In a thick-bottomed pan, heat the butter, and brown the meat on all sides. Remove from the pan, discard the butter and put the meat back into the pan. Add 12 of the garlic cloves, the thyme and half the wine. Cover with greaseproof paper and the lid, and put into the oven for 15 minutes, basting occasionally.

Lower the heat to 160ºC/Gas 3, and cook for a further 2 hours, basting every 20 minutes. Add more wine so there is always about 5mm liquid in the bottom of the pan.

After 2 hours, remove the lid and cook for 15 minutes to brown.

Toast the bread on each side, and rub lightly with garlic. Drizzle with olive oil.

The meat will fall into pieces off the bone. Tap out the marrow. Serve the meat with the juices and a crostini spread with the marrow.

'Ask your butcher to cut the ends off the veal shin bones to reveal the marrow.'

Veal loin, tomato, capers

Veal loin on the bone	2kg
Plum tomatoes	6
Flat-leaf parsley leaves	2 tbs
Garlic cloves	4
Capers	3 tbs
Unsalted butter	80g
Red wine vinegar	100ml

Preheat the oven to 150°C/Gas 2.

Season the meat on all sides. Skin, deseed and roughly chop the tomatoes (see page 66). Chop the parsley. Peel the garlic. Rinse the capers.

Melt the butter in a casserole. Brown the meat on all sides, then add the vinegar and let it reduce. Place in the preheated oven and roast for 1½ hours. Turn and baste the meat after the first half-hour. After an hour, add the garlic and, 5 minutes later, the tomatoes and 1 tbs sea salt. Continue to roast for a further 30 minutes, then add the capers and parsley, and stir into the tomato sauce.

Carve the veal on the bone as a thick chop with the sauce spooned over.

'The tradition of adding sweet, ripe tomatoes to the roast veal pan instead of wine to make the sauce comes from Campania in Southern Italy. Adding salted capers to the sauce was suggested to us by our Neopolitan friend, Antonella.'

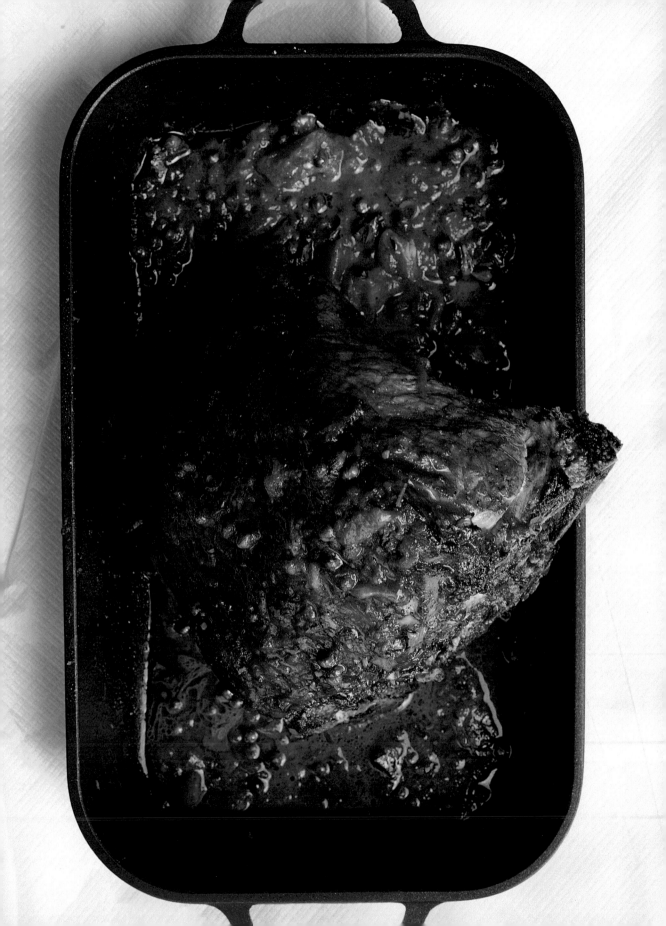

Cold roast veal, fresh tomato

Cold roast veal	500g
Tomato sauce	250ml
Basil leaves	2 tbs
Salted capers	50g
Lemons	2
Ex. v. olive oil	

Make the Tomato sauce (see page 67) and allow to cool. Wash the basil, and rinse the capers.

Slice the veal as finely as possible. Squeeze the juice of 1 lemon and mix it with three times its volume of olive oil. Season.

Lay the veal slices over each plate. Season with sea salt, and drizzle with the dressing. Spoon over the tomato sauce, and scatter with the capers and basil leaves. Drizzle with olive oil.

'This is the southern version of vitello tonnato, a summer dish that is refreshing as well as filling. The recipe comes from Puglia. Leftover cold pork would work just as well.'

Cold roast pork, mayonnaise

Cold roast pork	500g
Lemons	2
Capers	30g
Anchovy fillets	6
Parsley leaves	2 tbs
Egg yolks, organic	2
Ex. v. olive oil	

Finely slice the cold pork. Squeeze the juice of both lemons. Rinse the capers. Rinse the anchovies, then drizzle 1 tsp lemon juice over them and chop. Finely chop the parsley.

To make the mayonnaise, whisk the egg yolks with 1 tsp lemon juice, then add 250ml olive oil drop by drop until you have a thick sauce. Stir in the capers, anchovies and parsley. Taste for seasoning.

Mix the remaining lemon juice with 3 times its volume of olive oil, season.

Lay the pork out on a large serving plate, season and drizzle with dressing. Spoon over the mayonnaise. Serve with lemon.

'This recipe is similar to Milanese vitello tonnato in that the pork is thinly sliced and covered with mayonnaise, flavoured here with anchovies and capers rather than the traditional tuna.'

Beef fillet, red wine, horseradish

Beef fillet	1.5kg
Fresh horseradish	100g
Crème fraîche	150ml
Red wine vinegar	1 tbs
Ex. v. olive oil	1 tbs
Rosemary sprigs	2
Red wine	350ml
Unsalted butter	100g

Preheat the oven to 200°C/Gas 6.

Trim and season the beef fillet. Peel the horseradish, grate finely, then add the crème fraîche, red wine vinegar and season.

Heat the olive oil in a saucepan large enough to hold the fillet. Brown the meat well on all sides. Add the rosemary, cover with greaseproof paper, place in the preheated oven, and roast for 15 minutes.

Remove the beef. Add the red wine to the pan, and reduce by half over a medium heat, scraping up the juices. Whisk in the butter.

Cut the beef into thick slices, and spoon over the sauce. Serve with the horseradish.

'When choosing beef fillet, the outer flesh should be a bright purplish-red colour laced with thin streaks of white fat. The steak should be firm to the touch and not at all wet. When cut into portions the meat should have a fine texture and scarlet colour.'

Twelve-hour beef shin

For 6

Beef shin on the bone	3kg
Garlic cloves	50
Chianti Classico	750ml
Thyme sprigs	8
Ground black pepper	3 tbs
Ex. v. olive oil	
Sourdough loaf	½

Ask your butcher to cut a section across the shin, so that you have the sawn-off bone surrounded by meat as for ossobuco, but here with beef. You will have one largeish piece, which will be enough for 6.

Preheat the oven to 70°C/ the very lowest gas.

Peel the garlic cloves.

Place the piece of beef in an ovenproof dish with a tight-fitting lid. Cover with the wine, and add the garlic, thyme, pepper and a little salt. Slowly bring to the boil, then cover with greaseproof paper. Put on the lid and cook in the preheated oven for 12 hours. Take a look every 4 hours and top up the wine if the beef is uncovered. You may use more than 1 bottle of wine. Test for seasoning.

Cut the bread into thick slices, toast on both sides. Serve chunks of meat on top with the garlic and the juices. Drizzle with olive oil.

'This extreme recipe is based on the recipe for Peposo alla Fornacina, a dish from the area around the village of Panzano. Their flamboyant butcher, Dario Cecchini,who often serves plates of Peposo to his customers, introduced us to the dish, which was traditionally left to cook in the bread oven overnight.'

10

Grilled
fish & meat

Flattened sardine, chilli, lemon

Sardines	16
Dried chillies	4
Lemons	5
Ex. v. olive oil	

To flatten the sardines, cut off the head, and then prise the sardines open. Press down to loosen the bone, then remove from the flesh, pulling gently with your fingers.

Crumble the chillies. Finely grate the zest of 3 lemons; halve the rest.

Preheat the barbecue, griddle pan or grill.

Rub the flesh of the sardines with chilli, salt, pepper and lemon zest. Place skin-side down on the preheated grill, and cook for 1-2 minutes. Turn over and grill flesh-side down for a further 1-2 minutes.

Drizzle with olive oil, and serve with lemon.

'This simple method of grilling boned, flattened small fish can also be applied to fresh anchovies, baby red mullet and baby squid.'

Grilled fish & meat

Whole Dover sole

Dover sole	4 x 500g
Lemons	2
Ex. v. olive oil	

Ask your fishmonger to skin the Dover sole on both sides. Halve the lemons.

Preheat the barbecue, griddle pan or grill.

Season the sole generously on both sides, and brush lightly with olive oil. Place the fish on the very hot grill for 2-3 minutes, then turn over and grill the other side for another 2 minutes, or until the fish is cooked.

Serve with lemon and a drizzle of olive oil.

'The Dover sole season is from May to September/October when the water starts to cool. Flatfish flesh changes as the fish begin to roe at this time, the consequence being that the fish are thinner and softer, and not good to cook.'

Grilled fish & meat

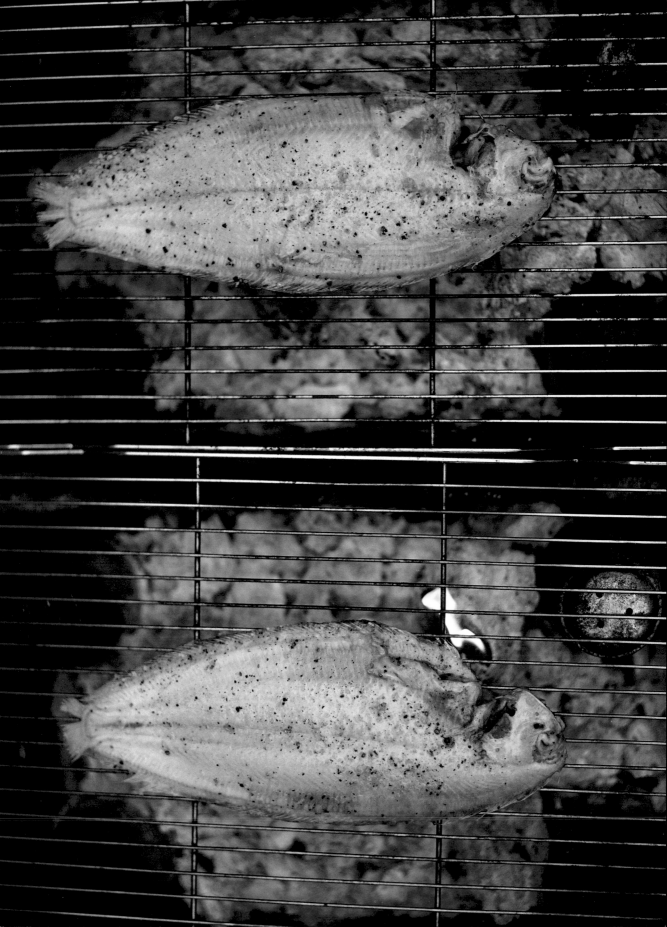

Whole side of salmon

For 8

Wild salmon side	1
Ex. v. olive oil	
Lemon	1

Ask the fishmonger to trim and fillet a whole side of wild salmon. Leave the skin on. Season both sides of the salmon and rub with olive oil. Quarter the lemon.

Preheat a barbecue, griddle pan or grill.

Place the salmon skin-side down on the grill. Cook for 4 minutes. Turn over and grill for a further 3 minutes. The fish should be rare in the middle.

Place on a platter skin-side up. Drizzle with olive oil and cut into thick slices. Serve with lemon.

'This is a party dish so it is worth getting hold of a side of wild salmon. Grill ideally on a large barbecue, over low coals. If you are grilling on a grill pan, cut the fillet to fit. It's important that the salmon is brushed with olive oil on both sides, to avoid the risk of sticking.

Salsa verde is delicious with all grilled fish (see page 131).'

Baby squid, marjoram

Baby squid	600g
Lemons	2
Marjoram leaves	3 tbs
Dried chillies	2
Ex. v. olive oil	

Clean the squid by pulling away the head and tentacles, along with the soft pulp inside the sac. Cut out the hard beak. Wash the tentacles and the sac, inside and out. Keep the skin and fins on. Pat dry. Squeeze the juice of 1 lemon; cut the second into quarters. Roughly chop the marjoram, and crumble the chillies.

Preheat a barbecue, griddle pan or grill.

Season the squid generously, inside and out, and push 1 tsp of the marjoram inside each sac.

Mix the crumbled chilli with 1 tsp lemon juice, 2 tbs olive oil and the remaining marjoram.

Place the squid bodies and tentacles on the hot grill briefly, and squeeze over a little lemon juice. Turn almost immediately, when the white flesh is lightly charred, and char the other side. Serve with the sauce and lemon.

'The smaller the squid, the more tender they will be. For this recipe, choose squid with bodies no longer than 8cm.'

Halibut on the bone

Halibut steaks	4
Ex. v. olive oil	
Lemons	2

Lightly season the halibut steaks on both sides, and brush with olive oil. Cut the lemons in quarters.

Preheat the barbecue, griddle pan or grill.

Place the halibut on the medium-hot grill and cook for 2 minutes, or until the fish comes away easily from the grill and is lightly browned. Turn over and grill on the other side for another 2 minutes.

Squeeze over a little lemon juice and serve with salsa verde (see page 131).

'For this recipe, the halibut steaks need to be cut 2-3cm thick. Choose steaks with very white flesh and be careful not to grill for too long as they cook quickly and will become dry.'

Grilled fish & meat

Bass brushed
with rosemary

Sea bass	**3kg**
Lemons	**2**
Rosemary branches	**2**
Ex. v. olive oil	

Halve the lemons.

Preheat the barbecue, griddle pan or grill.

Season the inside of the fish. Put 1 rosemary branch in the cavity, and lightly rub oil over the fish, especially on the tail. Season.

Put 6 tbs olive oil in a small bowl. Place the fish on the preheated grill and brush the fish, using the second rosemary branch dipped in the oil. Turn over after 8 minutes, brush again, season, and cook for a further 8 minutes.

Put the fish on a serving plate, serve with lemon.

'The grill should always be very hot before starting to cook to prevent the fish from sticking. Coating the fish with olive oil, paying special attention to the tail end, and rubbing with salt and pepper also helps.'

Flattened quail, chilli, salt

Organic quail	12
Dried chillies	4
Thyme sprigs	24
Lemons	2
Sea salt	4 tbs
Ex. v. olive oil	

Preheat the barbecue, griddle pan or grill.

Crumble the chilli. Halve the lemons.

Dry the quail with kitchen paper, and lay breast-side down on a board. With a pair of scissors, cut out the backbone and discard. Press and flatten the bird.

Rub with sea salt and dried chilli.

Place the quails on the preheated grill breast-side down, scatter over the thyme and grill for at least 5 minutes. Turn and cook for a further 5 minutes.

Serve with a drizzle of olive oil and the lemon.

'Free range quail are slightly larger with much more flavour than farmed quail but they are hard to find. Don't bother trying to flatten the tiny, farmed quail – they are too small and will dry up on the grill.'

Grilled fish & meat

Lamb chop, bruschetta

Lamb cutlets	16
Sourdough loaf	¼
Garlic clove	1
Lemons	2
Rosemary branch	1
Ex. v. olive oil	

Ask your butcher for best-end cutlets with the bones trimmed of fat and skin. Cut the bread into 4 thick slices. Peel the garlic. Cut the lemons into quarters.

Preheat the barbecue, griddle pan or grill.

Season the chops on both sides. Place on the grill and brown on each side, about 3 minutes. Squeeze a little lemon juice over whilst grilling.

Grill the sourdough slices on both sides, and rub one side lightly with the garlic. Rub the same side with the rosemary, then drizzle with olive oil.

Serve the chops with the bruschetta, a piece of the rosemary and some lemon.

'This is great to do on a barbecue, to be enjoyed eating with your fingers. Carefully trim all the fat from the chops, especially around the bone, as it will flame up and blacken on the barbecue, spoiling the flavour.'

Grilled fish & meat

Thick-cut sirloin, horseradish

Sirloin steak	**1.2kg**
Fresh horseradish	**100g**
Red wine vinegar	**3 tbs**
Ex. v. olive oil	

Cut the fat from the back of the sirloin steak and cut it lengthways into approximately 2 x 6cm thick steaks. Peel the horseradish.

Preheat the barbecue, griddle pan or grill.

Season the steaks on both sides, then place on the preheated grill for 1 minute to seal them. Turn over and seal the other side. Continue to grill, turning the steaks to prevent burning, for a further 5-6 minutes for medium-rare.

Slice the steaks as in the picture, and serve with a small pile of horseradish finely grated at the last minute. Drizzle some vinegar over the horseradish, and some olive oil over the steak.

'Fresh horseradish oxidises very quickly, which is why we suggest grating it at the very last minute.'

11

Italian vegetables

Fried aubergine, basil, tomato

Aubergines	2
Plum tomatoes	6
Garlic cloves	2
Ex. v. olive oil	
Basil leaves	3 tbs
Sunflower oil	250ml
Red wine vinegar	3 tbs

Wash the aubergines and cut into fine slices 3mm thick. Lay them on kitchen paper and sprinkle with sea salt. Make a cut in the tomato skin, blanch in boiling salted water for 30 seconds, and remove to cold water. Peel off the skins, cut each in half, and then in half again. Peel the garlic and slice in half. Wash the basil.

Heat 2 tbs olive oil in a thick-bottomed saucepan. Add the garlic and brown lightly, then add 1 tbs basil and the tomatoes. Season and cook for 15 minutes. The sauce should be thick.

Pat the salt off the aubergines. Heat half the sunflower oil in a large flat frying pan. When very hot, add a layer of aubergine slices. Fry briefly on each side to a light brown. Drain on kitchen paper. Continue frying, adding more oil to the pan if necessary.

To serve, lay the aubergine slices on a large plate, and sprinkle with vinegar. Spoon the tomato sauce over, but not to cover the aubergine completely, then scatter with the remaining basil leaves.

Italian vegetables

Roast aubergine, tomato

Aubergines	2
Plum tomatoes	8
Parmesan	100g
Basil leaves	2 tbs
Ex. v. olive oil	

Wash the aubergines, then cut off the stalks and the base. Slice into 2cm thick discs. Place them in a colander and sprinkle with sea salt. Leave for half an hour then pat dry.

Preheat the oven to 200°C/Gas 6.

Cut the tomatoes in half, squeeze out the juice, and chop the flesh into small pieces. Grate the Parmesan. Tear the basil into pieces.

Place the tomato in a bowl, add seasoning, and toss with 1 tbs of the oil, the Parmesan and basil.

Brush an ovenproof dish with olive oil. Place the aubergine slices on the dish, brush with olive oil and season. Bake in the preheated oven for 15 minutes. Turn over and spoon the tomato mixture on top. Return to the oven for 5 minutes.

'Of the many baked aubergine recipes in Southern Italian cooking, this one differs in mixing the grated Parmesan and the chopped tomato. The aubergines are best eaten warm.'

Roast whole pepper, capers

Red peppers	2
Yellow peppers	2
Ex. v. olive oil	
Marjoram leaves	3 tbs
Salted capers	50g
Red wine vinegar	2 tbs

Preheat the oven to 210°C/Gas 6.

Wash and dry the peppers and brush with olive oil, place on a tray and bake in the preheated oven until beginning to blister. Turn over and continue to bake, about 30 minutes in all. Cool the peppers in a bowl covered with clingfilm to keep in the moisture. Open the peppers up, peel and deseed when cool enough to handle.

Wash, dry and chop the marjoram. Rinse and chop the capers, and mix with the vinegar.

Lay the peppers out on a serving dish, and season. Sprinkle with vinegar and capers, scatter over the marjoram, and drizzle with olive oil.

'In Puglia, they roast the peppers whole in a very hot oven, usually a wood-burning pizza oven, until the skins blister. This method softens and sweetens the peppers, and makes them easy to peel.'

Zucchini scapece

Zucchini	600g
Garlic cloves	2
Mint leaves	2 tbs
Dried chillies	2
Sunflower oil	250ml
Red wine vinegar	3 tbs

Wash the zucchini, cut into 5mm thick ovals, and then cut each oval into thick matchsticks. Place in a colander, sprinkle with sea salt, and leave for half an hour. Peel and slice the garlic as finely as possible. Wash the mint. Crumble the chilli.

Heat the oil in a high-sided pan to 190°C or until a piece of zucchini browns immediately.

Pat the zucchini dry. Fry in the hot oil in batches until lightly brown. Drain on kitchen paper. Fry the mint for 2 seconds only. Drain. Serve the zucchini in a dish with the vinegar, mint and garlic sprinkled over. Finally season with salt, pepper and dried chilli.

'This is a Southern Italian recipe for frying zucchini. In Naples, the zucchini are cut into fine discs and deep-fried, then sprinkled with vinegar, mint and raw garlic (this recipe is in The River Cafe Cook Book). In Puglia, the zucchini are cut into thick matchsticks – a good way to use up larger zucchini.'

Zucchini trifolati, tomato

Zucchini	500g
Cherry tomatoes	300g
Garlic cloves	2
Basil leaves	2 tbs
Ex. v. olive oil	

Wash the zucchini and cut in half lengthways and then into rough pieces of about 2cm. Tear the tomatoes in half and squeeze out some of the seeds and juice. Peel and cut the garlic into slivers. Chop the basil.

Heat 2 tbs olive oil in a frying pan. Add the zucchini and garlic, and stir to combine. When the zucchini begin to brown, add the tomatoes, salt and pepper. Stir well, and cook for a further 5 minutes.

Remove from the heat and add the basil. Drizzle with extra virgin olive oil and cover. Let sit for at least 10 minutes before serving.

'Vegetables 'trifolati' is a method of slicing and cooking with garlic, olive oil and parsley. Other ingredients such as mint, wine or chillies are sometimes added. In this recipe we add fresh, ripe tomatoes.'

Roast porcini caps and stalks

Fresh porcini	750g
Lemon	1
Ex. v. olive oil	

Preheat the oven to 220°C/Gas 7.

Cut the caps from the stalks. Carefully wipe the caps clean, and peel the stalks. Cut each stalk in half lengthways. Quarter the lemon.

Lay the caps and stalks on a baking tray and season generously with salt and pepper. Drizzle over olive oil and roast in the preheated oven until tender, about 10 minutes.

Serve with a piece of lemon.

'Porcini mushrooms are called *ceps* in France, *penny buns* in the UK and *Boletus edulis* in reference books. They are the most prized mushrooms in Italian cooking. Their flavour is best when the porcini are fresh and firm. The season starts at the end of summer and ends with the first frost. Use large porcini for this recipe.'

Fried porcini, parsley, garlic

Fresh porcini	1kg
Garlic cloves	4
Parsley leaves	2 tbs
Ex. v. olive oil	

Clean the porcini carefully with a damp cloth. Separate the stalks from the caps. Roughly chop the stalks and slice the caps into 1cm pieces. Peel and finely chop the garlic. Chop the parsley.

Heat a large thick-bottomed frying pan, and add 2 tbs olive oil, then the porcini. Shake the pan over a high heat until the porcini begin to brown. Lower the heat, add the parsley and garlic, and continue to cook for at least 5 minutes. Season.

Drizzle with olive oil, and serve.

'The stalks of porcini have an excellent flavour and texture. This recipe is great for using the smaller mushrooms and any broken pieces. Do not undercook porcini, as they gain flavour from cooking.'

Smashed cannellini, olives

Dried cannellini beans	150g
Bicarbonate of soda	1 tbs
Dried chillies	2
Young spinach	500g
Garlic cloves	2
Sage leaves	2 tbs
Small black olives	100g
Ex. v. olive oil	

Soak the beans overnight with the bicarbonate of soda.

Crumble the chillies. Wash the spinach and remove any tough stalks. Peel the garlic.

Rinse the beans under cold water. Put the beans in a saucepan with the garlic and sage leaves, cover with water and bring to the boil. Skim off any scum, and simmer for 30 minutes. Add 1 tbs of sea salt and cook until tender, about 45 minutes in total. Drain, keep the garlic, discard the sage. Add 3 tbs olive oil,and roughly smash the beans and garlic. Season with half the chilli and black pepper.

Boil the spinach in salted water for 3 minutes, then drain. Press gently to remove excess moisture. Whilst warm, season and mix in 1 tbs olive oil.

Heat 2 tbs of olive oil, add the olives, some black pepper and a pinch of chilli. Fry for 1 minute.

Put the spinach and cannellini beans on plates with the olives over the top and a sprinkle of chilli.

'Try to find Taggiasca olives which come from the Ligurian coast of Italy. Usually preserved in brine, they are deep purple, small and have a fruity flavour. They are similar to Niçoise olives.'

Italian vegetables

Green bean, potato

Green beans	500g
New potatoes	500g
Flat-leaf parsley leaves	2 tbs
Garlic cloves	2
Ex. v. olive oil	

Top and tail the green beans. Scrub the skin off the potatoes. Chop the parsley finely. Peel the garlic and cut in half lengthways.

Put the potatoes into a saucepan, cover with cold water, add salt and cook until tender. Drain. Cook the green beans and garlic in boiling salted water until tender. Drain.

Mash the potatoes coarsely with a fork. Mix in 2 tbs olive oil, and season. Smash the green beans and garlic with a fork, then add 1 tbs olive oil and the parsley, and season.

Combine the potatoes and beans roughly. Drizzle over more olive oil, and serve.

'This is delicious in the summer, made with new potatoes and fresh green beans. It is really just a method of smashing them together with a fork and combining them with the olive oil. As the new potatoes are less floury, they remain firm and distinct.'

Half-mashed potato, parsley

Waxy potato	**750g**
Garlic cloves	**2**
Flat-leaf parsley leaves	**5 tbs**
Ex. v. olive oil	

Peel the potatoes, and cut each into 4 pieces lengthways. Peel the garlic. Chop the parsley finely.

Put the potatoes in a saucepan with the garlic, cover with cold water and cook for 15 minutes or until the potatoes are soft. Drain and season generously whilst hot.

Add 150ml of the best-quality extra virgin olive oil and the chopped parsley. Stir in the pan, half breaking the potatoes into a mash.

'This delicious recipe for simple mashed potatoes is designed to show off strong, peppery extra virgin olive oil. We had it first at the wine and olive oil estate, Capezzana, in Tuscany where they prepared a November lunch around their newly pressed oil. Adding parsley cleverly deepens the greenness of the olive oil and gives texture to the mashed potatoes.'

Fennel, tomato

Fennel bulbs	6
Garlic cloves	4
Dried chillies	2
Lemon	1
Tin tomatoes	400g
Ex. v. olive oil	

Trim off the tough outer stems and stalk of the fennel, then cut each bulb in half, and each half into sixths. Keep any of the green tops. Peel and slice the garlic cloves in half lengthways. Crumble the chillies. Squeeze the juice of the lemon.

Heat 2 tbs olive oil in a medium thick-bottomed saucepan, add the fennel and, after 2-3 minutes, the garlic. Stir to coat and prevent browning. Add the tomatoes, sea salt and chilli, stir and cover with a lid. Turn the heat down to low and gently cook for 20 minutes or until the fennel is soft and the tomatoes are absorbed into the fennel.

Chop the remaining green fennel and add with the lemon juice and 1 tbs olive oil to the pan.

'The most tender Florence fennel is in the shops from December through to March. The bulbs should be round, firm and white with feathery green shoots. Thinner, green fennel bulbs will be tough and fibrous and not suitable for this recipe.'

Roast celeriac, squash, fennel

Celeriac	250g
Butternut squash	250g
Fennel bulbs	2
Garlic cloves	4
Plum tomatoes	200g
Ex. v. olive oil	100ml

Preheat the oven to 200°C/Gas 6.

Peel then cut the celeriac in 2cm pieces. Peel the squash, scrape out the seeds, and cut into 1cm slices. Peel off the tough outer leaves of the fennel, cut each bulb in half, and then each half into 3 wedges. Peel the garlic cloves and cut in half. Cut the tomatoes in half.

Cook the celeriac and fennel in boiling salted water for 5 minutes. Drain and put in a large bowl. Add the squash, tomatoes and garlic. Season generously, and add the olive oil. Stir together to evenly coat the vegetables.

Place in a baking tray and roast in the preheated oven for half an hour. Turn the pieces over and continue to roast until all the vegetables are soft, possibly up to 45 minutes in total.

Cavolo nero, fennel seed

Cavolo nero	1kg
Garlic cloves	3
Fennel seeds	1 tsp
Dried chillies	2
Ex. v. olive oil	

Strip the leaves of the cavolo off the centre stem, wash. Peel the garlic and finely slice 2 of the garlic cloves. Crush the fennel seeds, and crumble the chillies.

Cook the cavolo in boiling salted water with the whole garlic clove until tender, about 5 minutes, then drain. Roughly chop it, including the garlic.

Heat 2 tbs olive oil in a thick-bottomed saucepan, and add the sliced garlic, chilli and fennel seeds. Fry until brown, about 2 minutes. Add the cavolo, season, and stir together briefly.

'When buying cavolo nero look for dark green leaves which are tightly crinkled and stiff. The correct flavour develops after the plants have had a few weeks of frost.

Be sure to boil the cavolo until it is very tender. Drain gently, retaining some of the water in the leaves so that it is juicy rather than fried with the olive oil.'

Broad bean, pea, asparagus

Broad beans in pod	500g
Peas in pod	500g
Asparagus	250g
Waxy potatoes	100g
Garlic cloves	2
Ex. v. olive oil	
Mint leaves	3 tbs

Pod the broad beans and peas. Snap off the tough stalks from the ends of the asparagus and cut the remainder into 1cm pieces, including the tips. Peel the potatoes and cut in 1cm cubes. Peel the garlic; keep whole.

Heat 3 tbs of olive oil in a thick-bottomed saucepan, and add the garlic, potato and broad beans. Stir together and cook for 5 minutes, then add the asparagus, peas and 200ml hot water. Season, and simmer for 20 minutes or until the liquid has been absorbed and the vegetables are cooked. Add more water if necessary.

Chop the mint and stir in, adding a drizzle of olive oil.

'Stewing spring vegetables together in olive oil is Roman in origin. There are many possible combinations – artichokes could replace the potatoes in this recipe, and spring onions could replace the asparagus. All recipes include fresh mint and extra virgin olive oil is drizzled over at the end.

Use frozen peas and broad beans if you need to save time.'

12

Baked fruit

Blackberries, mascarpone
Black fig, almond
Apricot, molasses, ginger
Apple, orange, walnut
Plum, vanilla, bruschetta
Whole pear, cinnamon
Quince, brown sugar
Rhubarb, orange

Blackberries, mascarpone

Blackberries	1kg
Vanilla pods	2
Mascarpone	500g
Egg yolks, organic	3
Icing sugar	30g

Preheat the oven to 200°C/Gas 6.

Wash and pick over the blackberries. Scrape the seeds from the vanilla pods. Separate the eggs.

Mix the mascarpone, egg yolks, vanilla seeds and sugar together.

Put the blackberries in a small baking dish. Spoon the mascarpone over and bake in the preheated oven until the mascarpone begins to brown, about 5 minutes.

'Mascarpone is a very rich, triple cream cheese from Lombardy in Northern Italy. It is used for savoury dishes as well as desserts. When heated, mascarpone melts into a creamy sauce. It keeps for at least a week in the fridge.'

Black fig, almond

Black figs	12
Blanched almonds	100g
Lemon	1
Brown sugar	2 tbs
Crème fraîche	150g

Preheat the oven to 150°C/Gas 2.

Split the almonds. Make a cross slash on the top of each fig, and squeeze from the bottom to open. Butter a shallow baking dish large enough to fit the figs. Squeeze the juice from the lemon.

Place the figs in the baking dish, and pour over the lemon juice. Sprinkle over the sugar and almonds.

Bake in the preheated oven for 10 minutes. Spoon over the juices, and bake for a further 5 minutes.

Serve warm with crème fraîche.

'Figs and almonds are a natural combination. Choose figs carefully – they should be soft but not squashed. Don't be tempted to eat figs out of season – they are best from June to September – or to buy under-ripe ones as they lack the flavour of tree-ripened figs.'

Apricot, molasses, ginger

Apricots	675g
Unsalted butter	50g
Fresh root ginger	50g
Lemon	1
Molasses	100g
Crème fraîche	150g

Preheat the oven to 180°C/Gas 4, and use some of the butter to grease a flat ovenproof dish.

Cut the apricots in half, and remove the stones. Peel and finely slice the ginger. Squeeze the lemon.

Lay the apricots out in the dish, cut-side up. Place a piece of the ginger on each apricot, with a small knob of butter and 1 tsp molasses. Sprinkle with lemon juice.

Place in the preheated oven and bake for 30 minutes.

Serve with crème fraîche.

'Since Roman times, ginger has been used as a spice in Southern Italian cooking, where it is often added to sauces, ice creams and cakes. This combination of tangy ginger slices with sweet, ripe apricots and dark molasses sugar is unusual but works well.'

Apple, orange, walnut

Oranges	2
Caster sugar	200g
Shelled walnuts	100g
Apples	4
Unsalted butter	50g
Crème fraîche	150g

Grate the zest of 1 orange and squeeze the juice. Cut up the second orange, and pound in a mortar. Push this through a sieve and keep the bitter pulp.

Put the sugar in a small saucepan, with enough water to just cover. Gently melt the sugar into a syrup, then add the zest and pulp of the oranges. Turn up the heat and boil to a caramel.

Wet a small oval dish with a spray of water. Place in the walnuts, and pour over the caramel. Leave to cool and set hard. Turn out and crack up the caramel into 2-3cm pieces.

Preheat the oven to 160°C/Gas 3.

Core the apples, and peel around the top third of the apples. Stuff the caramel and a little butter into the holes. Butter an ovenproof dish, and put the apples in it. Scatter any spare caramel pieces around. Pour in the orange juice, lightly cover with foil, and bake in the preheated oven for 45 minutes.

Serve with crème fraîche.

'It is important to use hard green baking apples such as Bramley.'

Plum, vanilla, bruschetta

Plums	500g
Vanilla pods	2
Caster sugar	200g
Sourdough loaf	¼
Unsalted butter	100g
Crème fraîche	150g
Lemon	1

Preheat the oven to 180°C/Gas 4.

Cut the plums in half and remove the stones. Chop 1 vanilla pod and mix with the caster sugar. Split open the second. Cut the bread into 4 x 1cm slices.

Butter an ovenproof dish thickly and place in the plums, cut-side up. Scatter over half of the vanilla sugar mix. Bake in the preheated oven for 15 minutes.

Butter the bread, and scatter over the remaining vanilla sugar mix. Place in the baking dish, piling the half-cooked plums over. Squeeze the juice from the lemon, cut into quarters and put in the pan. Continue to bake for a further 15 minutes. The bread should be slightly crisp at the edges, and soaked with the plums and their juices in the middle.

Serve with crème fraîche.

'When buying vanilla pods, choose nice fat ones. To make the vanilla flavour more powerful, chop some of the pods with the caster sugar before adding them to the plums, keeping just a few whole to scatter over the top. Mix some of the inside vanilla seeds into the butter for the bruschetta if you are a real vanilla fan.'

Baked fruit

Whole pear, cinnamon

Pears	4
Unsalted butter	100g
Cinnamon sticks	2
Soft brown sugar	2 tbs
Grappa	200ml
Crème fraîche	150g
Vanilla pods	2

Preheat the oven to 150°C/Gas 2.

Wash the pears. Cut a small slice from the bottom of each pear so that they will stand in the dish. Butter a baking dish that will hold the pears. Break the cinnamon in half, split the vanilla pods.

Rub some butter over each pear, place in the dish, and sprinkle over the sugar, vanilla and cinnamon sticks, and cover the dish with foil.

Bake in the preheated oven for 20 minutes, then remove the foil, add the grappa. Return to the oven and bake for a further 20 minutes or until the pears are very tender.

Serve warm with the juices and crème fraîche.

'Grappa is a strong spirit made from grape skins, seeds and pulp after the juice has been pressed out for wine-making. It can be made from a single grape variety (i.e. grappa di merlot) or a blend of varieties. Use a white grappa which will take on the pure flavour of the pears, not an oak-aged, golden one.'

Quince, brown sugar

Quince	2
Lemon	1
Unsalted butter	100g
Soft brown sugar	150g
Crème fraîche	150g

Preheat the oven to 160°C/Gas 3.

Brush the down from the quince, cut in half, and cut out the cores. Cut the lemon in half.

Thickly butter an ovenproof dish. Scatter the sugar over, reserving 4tsp. Put a knob of butter and a tsp of sugar in each core cavity and place the quince in the dish, cut-side down. Squeeze over a little lemon juice, and bake in the preheated oven for 30 minutes, or until soft.

Serve with the juices and crème fraîche.

'Choose ripe quince that are yellow and firm, not soft ones which are likely to be rotten in the centre. Brush the down from the skin before baking. There are many varieties of quince: the smaller varieties which are usually found in England are most suitable for baking.'

Baked fruit

Rhubarb, orange

Champagne rhubarb	500g
Blood orange	1
Vanilla pods	2
Demerara sugar	3 tbs
Crème fraîche	150g

Preheat the oven to 150°C/Gas 2.

Cut the rhubarb into 5-6cm lengths. Finely grate the zest of half the orange, then squeeze the juice. Split the vanilla pods, and scrape out some of the seeds.

Lay the rhubarb pieces flat in a small baking dish. Scatter over the vanilla seeds, sugar and orange zest. Add the vanilla pods. Pour over the orange juice and bake in the preheated oven for 15-20 minutes.

Serve with crème fraîche.

'Champagne rhubarb is the first bright pink rhubarb to appear in the shops around the end of January. It is a forced variety and is tender and sweet – you hardly need to do anything to it other than add brown sugar. We also add a little orange zest and juice – a classic combination.'

13

Lemon puddings

Lemon, mascarpone tart

Sweet pastry

Unsalted butter	225g
Eggs, organic	3
Plain flour	350g
Salt	½ tsp
Icing sugar	100g

Filling

Lemons	6
Eggs, organic	6
Egg yolks, organic	6
Caster sugar	350g
Mascarpone	300g
Icing sugar	2 tbs

For the pastry, cut the cold butter into small pieces. Separate the eggs. In a food processor, pulse-chop the flour, salt and butter to the texture of coarse breadcrumbs. Add the icing sugar and egg yolks and pulse into a soft ball. Wrap in cling film and chill for 1 hour.

Preheat the oven to 150°C/Gas 2.

Coarsely grate the pastry into a loose-bottomed, fluted 26cm flan tin, then press it evenly to cover the sides and base. Line with greaseproof paper and fill with baking beans. Bake blind for 20 minutes. Cool. Reduce the oven to 140°C/Gas 1.

For the filling, grate the lemon zest, squeeze the juice, and mix together. Beat the eggs and yolks with the sugar. Add the mascarpone, and stir to combine, then stir in the lemon mixture.

Pour into the tart shell, and bake for an hour. Cool, and sprinkle over the icing sugar.

Lemon, ricotta, pine nut cake

Lemons	3
White breadcrumbs	80g
Ricotta	600g
Caster sugar	200g
Eggs, organic	4
Egg yolks, organic	2
Crème fraîche	200g
Mascarpone	350g
Lemon essence	2 tbs
Pine nuts	50g

Preheat the oven to 150°C/Gas 2.

Butter the sides and bottom of a 25cm springform cake tin.

Finely grate the lemon zest, squeeze the juice and combine. Leave for 10 minutes to infuse. Make the breadcrumbs (see page 277).

Whisk the ricotta with the sugar until smooth. Add the eggs and egg yolks one at a time and continue beating. Add the crème fraîche. Finally, fold in the lemon mixture and mascarpone, and add the lemon essence.

Shake the tin with the breadcrumbs to evenly coat all sides. Pour in the cake mixture, shake over the pine nuts and bake for 45 minutes in the preheated oven until just set but wobbly. Cool and turn out.

'Pine nuts can rapidly become rancid due to their high oil content, so buy only small amounts and always check the use-by date.

This is a Tuscan variation of the *Torta della Nonna*, a traditional cake made at Easter with raisins and pastry.'

Lemon puddings

Lemon, almond cake

Lemons	4
Caster sugar	200g
Egg yolks, organic	5
Unsalted butter	150g
Ground almonds	300g
Self-raising flour	100g
Egg whites, organic	3
Baking powder	2 tsp

Preheat the oven to 180°C/Gas 4.

Use extra butter and flour to line a 22 x 11cm tin.

Finely grate the zest of the lemons and squeeze the juice. Put both in a bowl, and add the sugar and egg yolks. Put in a saucepan and cook gently, stirring, over a very low heat until thick. Stir in the softened butter. Strain through muslin and cool.

Add the ground almonds and flour to the lemon mixture.

Beat the egg whites to soft peaks. Fold in the baking powder and then combine with the lemon and almond mixture.

Pour into the prepared tin, and bake in the preheated oven for 50 minutes. Allow to cool in the tin.

'In most of the cake recipes using lemon juice, we also include the grated rind. Buy unwaxed lemons for this, and wash and dry thoroughly before grating. This is a simple cake, delicious for breakfast, a time when Italians eat their desserts!'

Lemon semifreddo

Lemons	4
Eggs, organic	4
Caster sugar	200g
Double cream	250ml
Fine salt	1 tsp

Grate the zest and squeeze the juice of the lemons, and mix together. Separate the eggs.

Beat the egg yolks with the sugar in an electric mixer until light, for at least 8 minutes. Place the mixture in a bowl over a large saucepan of simmering water (do not let the bowl touch the water). Whisk continuously until the mixture comes to the boil. Cool, then add the lemon mixture. Lightly beat the cream and fold in. Beat the egg whites with the salt until stiff. Fold into the lemon and egg yolk mixture.

Line a tin that will fit in the freezer with greaseproof paper. Pour in the mixture and freeze until firm.

'Semifreddo is half-frozen ice cream, with whipped cream folded into the mixture to give a mousse-like texture.'

Lemon, apple cake

Lemons	2
Apples	4
Blanched almonds	125g
Butter	110g
Vanilla pod	1
Caster sugar	300g
Eggs, organic	2
Milk	150ml
Plain flour	5 tbs
Baking powder	1½ tsp

Preheat the oven to 150°C/Gas 2.

Line a 23cm cake tin with parchment paper and grease with extra butter.

Grate the lemon zest. Peel, core and slice the apples finely. Grind the almonds to a fine flour. Melt the butter. Split the vanilla pod, and scrape the seeds out. Mix with the sugar.

Beat the vanilla sugar and the eggs together until thick and light. Slowly add the milk and melted butter. Fold the almond flour into the plain flour, and then stir into the batter. Add the baking powder, lemon zest and three-quarters of the apple.

Pour into the prepared tin, put the remaining apple over the top, and scatter with 1 tbs of sugar. Bake in the oven for 1 hour.

Remove from the tin when cool.

'Maria Manetti makes this delicious cake for us every time we visit the lovely Fattoria Fontodi in Panzano. Golden Delicious is the variety of apple she uses.'

Lemon, vodka-Martini granita

Lemons	8
Ice cubes	8
Vodka	400ml
Sugar syrup	
Caster sugar	140g
Water	100ml

To make the sugar syrup, heat the sugar gently with the water until dissolved, then boil briefly until you have a light syrup. Cool.

Wash the lemons and grate the zest of 6 of them. Squeeze the juice of all 8. You should have about 500ml. Mix together the lemon juice with the zest, and leave for 30 minutes.

Roughly smash the ice. Mix the vodka with 100ml of the sugar syrup and the lemon mixture, add the ice and freeze in a tray until solid.

To serve, use a fork to scrape up the granita into Martini glasses.

'This vodka granita is a less alcoholic way of downing a Martini. Serve it at the end of a special meal instead of brandy or grappa.'

14

Chocolate & coffee

Bitter chocolate mousse cake

Sponge

Unsalted butter	100g
Caster sugar	100g
Eggs, organic	2
Plain flour	100g
Baking powder	2 tsp

Chocolate mousse

Chocolate 70%	175g
Eggs, organic	4
Caster sugar	115g
Strong coffee	3 tbs
Unsalted butter	175g

To serve

Brandy	80ml
Double cream	150ml
Cocoa powder	1 tbs

Preheat the oven to 150°C/Gas 2.

Use extra butter and flour to line a 22.5 x 11cm loaf tin.

For the sponge, cream the butter and sugar together until pale yellow. Add the eggs, one at a time. Fold in the flour and baking powder, and put into the tin. Bake for 15 minutes.

For the mousse, break the chocolate into pieces, and separate the eggs. Beat the egg yolks and 100g of the sugar until pale, about 5 minutes.

Melt the chocolate with the coffee in a bowl over hot water. Remove from the heat and stir in the butter, a little at a time. Add egg mixture.

Beat the egg whites to soft peaks. Add the remaining sugar and beat until stiff. Fold into the chocolate, cover. Chill for at least 2 hours.

Cut the sponge into horizontal slices 1cm thick. Line the bottom of the loaf tin with greaseproof paper, cover with a single layer of sponge. Drizzle with half the brandy and spoon in a layer of mousse. Line the sides of the tin with slices of sponge and fill with the remaining mousse, cover with sponge, drizzle with remaining brandy, press down. Cool for 1 hour.

Whip cream, spread over cake and top with cocoa powder.

Chocolate & coffee

Hazelnut truffle cake

Chocolate 70%	250g
Unsalted butter	120g
Shelled hazelnuts	200g
Demerara sugar	6 tbs
Dark rum	150ml
Eggs, organic	4
Double cream	250ml

Preheat the oven to 200ºC/Gas 6.

Butter the base of a 16cm springform cake tin. Line with parchment paper, and butter the paper.

Roast the hazelnuts for 10 minutes. Pulse-chop in a food processor until finely ground.

Melt the butter in a small thick-bottomed saucepan, add the sugar, and boil to lightly caramelise. Add the hazelnuts, stir until the nuts begin to stick together, about 2-3 minutes. Whilst warm, spread this mixture into the base of the tin.

Break the chocolate in pieces and melt with the rum in a bowl over simmering water. Cool.

Separate the eggs. Beat the egg yolks until pale. Stir into the chocolate then slowly add the cream. The mixture will thicken immediately. Spoon into the cake tin and leave to set for 1 hour in the fridge.

To remove from the tin, soak a cloth in hot water and wrap it around the tin for 1 minute to slightly melt the edges. Unclip the springform. Carefully slide the cake off the base on to a cake plate.

'This recipe comes from the restaurant Scacciapensieri, in Cecina, Tuscany.'

Chocolate & coffee

Coffee, walnut, hazelnut cake

Instant coffee	5 tbs
Shelled walnuts	240g
Shelled hazelnuts	240g
Vanilla pods	3
Unsalted butter	380g
Caster sugar	380g
Eggs, organic	5
Plain flour	100g
Baking powder	1 tsp

Preheat the oven to 160°C/Gas 3. Using extra butter and flour, grease a 25cm cake tin and line with parchment paper.

Dissolve the coffee in 2 tbs boiling water. Chop the walnuts. Roast the hazelnuts in the preheated oven until brown (about 10 minutes), cool, then rub off the skins and grind to a fine powder. Finely chop the vanilla pods.

Beat the butter and sugar together until pale and light. Stir in the hazelnuts, walnuts and vanilla pods. Beat the eggs into the mixture one at a time. Fold in the flour and baking powder and finally stir in the coffee.

Spoon into the prepared tin and bake in the preheated oven for 1¼ hours. Allow to cool on a rack.

'Using instant coffee in this recipe is intentional. The cake requires a very strong coffee flavour with as little liquid as possible, ruling out using filter or even espresso coffee.'

Chocolate vanilla truffles

Chocolate 70%	250g
Vanilla pods	2
Double cream	250ml

Coating

Chocolate 70%	200g
Cocoa powder 100%	50g

Chop the chocolate into small pieces. Put in a bowl. Split the vanilla pods.

Put the vanilla pods and cream into a saucepan and bring to the boil. Strain over the chocolate. Whisk gently until the chocolate has melted, cool.

When the mixture is firm, place the bowl over simmering water just to warm it through. Remove from the heat, and whisk well until smooth.

Put a sheet of parchment paper on a flat tray. Drop tablespoonfuls of the mixture on to the paper. Put in the fridge for an hour to set.

For the coating, melt the chocolate in a bowl over simmering water. Place the cocoa powder in a shallow dish.

Remove the truffles from the fridge. Dip the truffles into the melted chocolate and remove with a fork. Transfer to the cocoa powder and roll around to coat. Put in the fridge to harden for 15 minutes then into a sieve to shake off excess cocoa. Return to the fridge to harden further.

Tiramisu

Instant coffee	8 tbs
Brandy	300ml
Savoiardi biscuits	250g
Eggs, organic	2
Mascarpone	500g
Icing sugar	75g
Cocoa powder	25g

Make the instant coffee with 225ml hot water. Mix the coffee with the brandy.

Lay the biscuits out on a flat tray, and soak them in the coffee and brandy.

Separate the eggs. Mix the egg yolks into the mascarpone with the icing sugar. Beat the egg whites until soft peaks, then fold into the mascarpone.

Using an oval 35 x 24cm ceramic dish, make a layer of wet biscuits. Cover with a thick layer of mascarpone. Shake over some cocoa powder, then repeat with a further layer of biscuits and mascarpone. Shake over cocoa powder, and chill for a minimum of 2 hours before serving.

'There are endless versions of this modern dessert. Ours is very rich and wet with lots of alcohol and mascarpone.'

Pannacotta, chocolate

Double cream	1 litre
Vanilla pods	2
Gelatine leaves	2½
Milk	125ml
Icing sugar	125g
Chocolate sauce	
Chocolate 70%	300g
Unsalted butter	45g

Heat 750ml of the cream in a thick-bottomed pan. Add the vanilla, bring to the boil, and simmer to reduce by one-third. Remove the pods and scrape the seeds into the cream.

Soak the gelatine in the milk for 15 minutes. Remove the gelatine, then heat the milk until boiling. Return the gelatine to the milk and stir until dissolved. Add to the hot cream, and cool.

Whip the remaining cream with the icing sugar. Fold into the cooled cooked cream. Pour into four 200ml bowls, and allow to set in the fridge for 2 hours.

Break up the chocolate and melt with the butter in a bowl over simmering water.

Turn out the set creams on to plates, pour over the chocolate, and serve immediately. This has to be done at the last minute or the chocolate will stiffen.

'The pannacotta can be made the day before. The chocolate mixture can be kept warm in a double boiler. If you are feeling festive, pour a little grappa over the pannacotta before you pour over the chocolate!'

Chocolate, coffee sorbet

Strong coffee	**150ml**
Cocoa powder	**150g**
Caster sugar	**250g**

Bring 650ml water to the boil with the sugar and boil for 4 minutes. Allow to cool.

Add the coffee and cocoa powder, and cook over a low heat for 15 minutes, stirring to combine.

Strain and churn in an ice-cream machine, or freeze in a shallow container, stirring every half-hour or so.

'This sorbet is very easy to make and inexpensive. Espresso coffee is our first choice, but you can also use a very strong filter coffee made with a higher ratio of coffee to water.'

Rum, coffee truffle cake

Chocolate 70%	500g
Double cream	600ml
Instant coffee	3 tbs
Rum	200ml
Cocoa powder	3 tbs

Break the chocolate into pieces, and melt in a bowl over simmering water.

Warm the cream then dissolve the coffee in it. Stir this into the warm chocolate, with the rum.

Place a 15cm cake ring on a flat plate. Pour the mixture into the ring, and leave to set for 2 hours in the fridge.

To remove the ring, soak a dish cloth in very hot water and wrap it around the ring for 2 minutes to slightly melt the edges of the cake, making it easy to turn out.

Shake the cocoa powder over the top.

'We make this in The River Cafe for birthdays as the recipe is easily adapted for any number. It is simply a flavoured combination of melted bitter chocolate and cream.'

Chocolate, almond cake

Chocolate 70%	180g
Unsalted butter	180g
Blanched almonds	200g
Eggs, organic	8
Vanilla pod	1
Caster sugar	215g
Cocoa powder	60g
Salt	a pinch

Preheat the oven to 150°C/Gas 2.

Line a 23cm cake tin with greaseproof paper, and grease with extra butter.

Break the chocolate into pieces. Cut the butter up into pieces. Grind the almonds fine in a food processor. Keep 2 eggs whole, and separate the other 6. Chop the vanilla pod.

Melt the chocolate and butter together in a bowl over simmering water. Allow to cool. Beat together the 2 whole eggs with the 6 egg yolks and 200g of the sugar. Fold in the cocoa powder and ground almonds. Mix together with the melted chocolate, then stir in the chopped vanilla.

Beat 4 of the egg whites to stiff peaks with the salt. Fold in the remaining 15g sugar. Fold the whites gently into the chocolate mix.

Pour into the prepared tin and bake in the preheated oven for 25 minutes. Turn out when cool, and serve dusted with extra cocoa powder.

'We use unsweetened cocoa powder from Valrhona to dust the cake. Put the cocoa into a fine sieve and dust directly onto the surface of the cake. Do this just before serving.'

How to Make…

Wet polenta

Polenta flour	350g
Ex. v. olive oil	3 tbs
Parmesan	200g

Grate the Parmesan. Put the polenta flour in a jug.

In a thick-bottomed pan, bring 1.7l of water and 1 tsp of salt to the boil. Reduce heat to a simmer and slowly pour in the polenta flour in a steady stream, stirring with a whisk until completely blended.

As soon as it starts to bubble, reduce heat as low as possible and cook, stirring from time to time with a wooden spoon. This will take about 45 minutes.

The polenta is cooked when it falls away from the sides of the pan.

Stir in either olive oil or 150g of butter and the grated Parmesan. Serve immediately.

Dried chickpeas

Chickpeas	250g
Bicarbonate of soda	2 tsp
Garlic cloves	4
Celery heart	1
Dried chillies	2
Ex. v. olive oil	5 tbs
Potato	1

Soak the chickpeas overnight in cold water with 1 tsp bicarbonate of soda.

Remove the tough outer leaves of celery, wash, and cut the heart in half. Peel the garlic.

Drain the chickpeas, rinse well and put in a pan with the remaining bicarbonate of soda, garlic, and celery, and cover with water.

Bring to the boil, skimming off the foam that rises to the surface. Turn heat down and simmer for half an hour. Add the chilli, 1 tbs sea salt and 3 tbs of olive oil. Continue simmering for a further 15 minutes or until the chickpeas are tender. Cool with the vegetables in their liquid.

To use, drain off most of the liquid, mash the celery and garlic into the chickpeas. Check seasoning and add 2tbs of olive oil.

Dried Borlotti & Cannelini

Beans	250g
Bicarbonate of soda	2 tsp
Garlic	1 bulb
Sage branches	2
Plum tomato	1

Soak the beans overnight in a generous amount of water with the bicarbonate of soda. Cut the garlic bulb in half. Wash the sage and the tomato.

Drain the beans, rinse and put in a thick-bottomed saucepan with the tomato, sage and garlic. Cover with cold water, bring to the boil and simmer, removing any scum that comes to the surface. Cook for approximately 45 minutes or until the beans are very tender. Remove from the heat and let cool in the liquid. Season.

Breadcrumbs

Ciabatta loaf	**1**

Preheat the oven to 180ºC/Gas 4.

Cut the crust from the bread, stale bread is good. Tear the bread into small pieces and pulse-chop in the food processor to medium.

Line an oven tray with parchment paper, scatter over the breadcrumbs and bake for 10 minutes or until lightly crisp. Store in airtight jars.

Dried porcini

Dried porcini	40g
Garlic cloves	2
Unsalted butter	100g
Ex. v. olive oil	

Soak the porcini in 200ml of boiling water for 10 minutes.

Peel and finely slice the garlic.

Drain the porcini, reserving the water.

Rinse the porcini under a running tap. Cut off any hard bits and roughly chop. Strain the liquid through muslin.

Melt the butter in a thick-bottomed frying pan, add the garlic and fry until soft, then add the porcini. Cook, stirring for 5 minutes to combine the flavours then add 4 tbs of the porcini liquid. Simmer until the juice has been absorbed, then add the remainder of the liquid. Simmer until the liquid is reduced to a sauce and thick. Season.

Italian store cupboard

This is a basic list of store cupboard items that you will find useful when using the book. Included are items that keep in the cupboard for up to six months and also everyday fresh ingredients to stock up on once a week and keep in the fridge.

We suggest always keeping tinned tomatoes, and for quick soups good quality tinned cannellini and borlotti beans and various stock cubes (we use chicken but vegetable stock cubes are fine). Essentials to keep in the bottom of the fridge are red onions, celery, garlic, and a few fresh herbs such as flat-leaf parsley and basil in season.

Choose an olive oil for cooking, and an extra virgin single estate oil for bruschettas, soups, and drizzling.

Buy white sourdough bread with an open texture and crisp crust. In this book we have used 1kg loaves.

Cupboard

sea salt
black peppercorns
dried red chillies
bay leaves (fresh or dried)
dried oregano
fennel seeds
nutmeg
stock cubes

capers
anchovies
black olives
extra virgin olive oil
red wine vinegar
aged balsamic vinegar
white wine
red wine
dijon mustard

tinned tomatoes
cannellini beans
borlotti beans
chickpeas
dried porcini
lentils (Puy or Casteluccio)

plain flour
semolina flour
risotto rice
polenta
spaghetti
tagliatelle
short pasta

70% chocolate
blanched whole almonds

Fridge

unsalted butter
crème fraîche
Parmesan cheese
free range organic eggs
pancetta

garlic
red onions
celery
flat-leaf parsley
sage
basil
thyme
marjoram

Suppliers

Birmingham
Harvey Nichols
Food Market
The Mailbox
31/32 Wharfside Street
Birmingham B1 1RE
0121 616 6000
www.harveynichols.com

Bristol
Fresh and Wild
85 Queens Road
Bristol BS8 1QS
0117 910 5930

Cambridge
Cambridge
Cheese Company
All Saints Passage
Cambridge CB2 3LS
01223 328 672

Landins
21 High Street
Kimbolton, Huntingdon
Cambridgeshire PE28 0HB
01480 860231

Channel Isles
Sommelier Wine Co. Ltd
23 St George's Esplanade
St Peter Port
Guernsey GY1 2BG
01481 721 677

Dunell's Ltd
La Route de la Haule
Beaumont, St Peter, Jersey
JE3 7YD
01534 736418
www.dunells.com

Cheltenham
CheeseWorks
5 Regent Street
Cheltenham GL50 1HE
01242 255 022

Cornwall
Matthew Stevens & Son
Back Road East
St Ives
Cornwall TR26 1NW
01736 799392
www.mstevensandson.com

Devon
Effings
50 Fore Street
Totnes Devon TQ9 5RP
01803 863 435

Crebers of Tavistock
48 Brook Street
Tavistock, Devon PL19 0BH
01822 61 22 66

East Sussex
Beckworth's Deli
67 High Street
Lewes East Sussex BN7 1XG
01273 474 502

Trencherman & Turner
52 Grove Road
Little Chelsea
Eastbourne
East Sussex BN21 4UD
01323 737 535
www.trenchermanandturner.
co.uk

Lanes Deli & Pasta Shop
12b Meeting House Lane
Brighton, East Sussex
BN1 1HB
01273 723522

Exeter
Pipers Farm
27 Magdalen Road
Exeter
01392 274504
www.pipersfarm.com

Gloucestershire
Maby's Food and Wine
Digbeth Street
Stow-On-The-Wold,
Cheltenham,
Gloucestershire GL54 1BN
01451 870 071

Daylesford Organic
Farm Shop
Daylesford, near Kingham
Gloucestershire GL56 0YG
01608 731 700
www.daylesfordorganic.com

Kent
Williams & Brown
Delicatessen
28a Harbour Street
Whitstable, Kent CT5 1AH
01227 274507

Leeds
Beano Wholefoods
Workers Co-op
36 New Briggate
Leeds LS1 6NU
0113 2435737
www.beanowholefoods.co.uk

Harvey Nichols
Food Market
107-111 Briggate
Victoria Quarter,
Leeds LS1 6AZ
0113 204 8888

Leicester
Stones Deli
2-6 St. Martins Square
Leicester LE1 5DG
0116 261 4430

Lincolnshire
The Dutch Eel Company
The Hall Farm Cottage
Glebe Road
Great Carlton
Louth, Lincolnshire
LN11 8JX
01507 450793

Liverpool
No 7 Deli
15 Faulkner Street
Liverpool L8 7PU
0151 709 9633

London
Baker and Spice
54-56 Elizabeth Street
Belgravia,
London SW1W 9PB
020 7730 3033

47 Denyer Street
Chelsea, London SW3 2LX
020 7589 4734

75 Salusbury Road
Queen's Park,
London NW6 6NH
020 7604 3636
www.bakerandspice.com

Blagdens Fishmongers
65 Paddington Street
London W1U 4JQ
020 7935 8321
blagfish@vossnet.co.uk

Brindisa
32 Exmouth Market
London EC1 4QE
020 7713 1666

32 Borough Market
London SE1 9AH
020 7407 1036

Suppliers

Clarke's
24 Kensington
Church Street
London W8 4BH
020 7221 9225
www.sallyclarke.com

The Conran Shop
81 Fulham Road
London SW3 6RD
020 7589 7401

East Dulwich Deli
15-17 Lordship Lane
London SE22 8EW

The Fish Shop
at Kensington Place
201 Kensington
Church Street
London W8 7LX
020 7243 6626

Frank Godfrey Butchers
7 Highbury Park
Highbury, London N5 1QJ
020 7226 9904

Fresh and Wild
49 Parkway
Camden Town London
NW1 7PN
020 7428 7575

194 Old Street
London EC1V 9FR
020 7250 1708

305-311 Lavender Hill
Clapham Junction
London SW11 1LN
020 7585 1488

208-212 Westbourne Grove
Notting Hill
London W11 2RH
020 7229 1063

69-75 Brewer Street
Soho London W1F 9US
020 7434 3179

32-40 Stoke Newington
Church Street
Stoke Newington London
N16 0LU
020 7254 2332
www.freshandwild.com

Gazzano
167-169 Farringdon Road
London EC1R 3AL
020 7250 1002

The Ginger Pig
8-10 Moxon Street
London
W1U 4EW
020 7935 7788

Harrods Food Hall
Brompton Road
Knightsbridge London
SW1X 7XL
020 7730 1234

Harvey Nichols
Food Market
109-125 Knightsbridge
London SW1X 7RJ
020 7235 5000
www.harveynichols.com

La Fromagerie
30 Highbury Park
London N5 2SS
020 7359 7440

2-4 Moxon Street
London W1 4EW
020 7935 0341
www.lafromagerie.co.uk

Lidgate Butchers
110 Holland Park Avenue
London W11 4UA
020 7727 8243

Lina Stores
18 Brewer Street
London W1R 3FS
020 7437 6482

Luigi's
349 Fulham Road
London SW10 9TW
020 7352 7739

Montes Delicatessen
23A Canonbury Lane
London N1 2AS
020 7354 4335
www.montesdeli.com

Mortimer and Bennett
33 Turnham Green Terrace
London W4 1RG
020 8995 4145
www.mortimerandbennett.
co.uk

Neal's Yard Dairy
17 Shorts Garden
London WC2H 9AT
020 7645 3532

6 Park Street,
Borough Market
London SE1 9AB
020 7645 3554
www.nealsyarddairy.co.uk

Panzer's
13-19 Circus Road
London NW8 5PB
020 7722 8596
www.panzers.co.uk

Planet Organic
42 Westbourne Grove
London W2 5SH
020 7227 2227

25 Effie Road
Fulham, London SW6 1EL
020 7731 7222

22 Torrington Place
London WC1 7JE
020 7436 1929
www.planetorganic.com

Poilâne Bakery
42-46 Elizabeth Street
London SW1W 9PA
020 7808 4910
www.poilane.fr

Portobello Food Co.
020 8980 6664
www.portobellofood.com

The River Cafe
Thames Wharf
Rainville Road
London W6 9HA
020 7386 4200
www.rivercafe.co.uk

Rococo
321 King's Road
London SW3 5EP
020 7352 5857
www.rococochocolates.com

The Salusbury
56 Salusbury Road
London NW6 6NN
020 7328 3287

Speck Delicatessen
2 Holland Park Terrace,
Portland Road
Holland Park, London W11
020 7229 7005

6 Thayer Street
London W1
020 7486 4872

Tavola
155 Westbourne Grove
London W11 2RS
020 7229 0571

Vallebona
Unit 14, 59 Weir Street
London SW19 8UG
020 8944 5665
www.vallebona.co.uk

Villandry
170 Great Portland Street
London W1W 5QB
020 7631 3131
www.villandry.com

Manchester
Harvey Nichols
Food Market
Exchange Square
Manchester M1 1AD
0161 828 8888
www.harveynichols.com

Love Saves the Day
46-50 Oldham Street
Manchester M4 1LE
0161 832 0777
www.lovesavestheday.co.uk

Chorlton Wholefoods
34 Beech Road
Chorlton-Cum-Hardy
M21 1EL
01618 816 399

North Yorkshire
Archimboldo's Deli
146 King's Road
Harrogate,
North Yorkshire HG1 5HY
01423 508 760

Oxfordshire
Wells Stores
Peach Croft Farm
12 Acre Drive
Abingdon OX14 2HP
01235 535 978

Shrewsbury
Appleyards Deli
85 Wyle Cop
Shrewsbury SY1 1VT
01743 240 180

Somerset
The Olive Garden Deli
87 Hill Road
Clevedon
North Somerset B521 7TN
01275 341 222

Southampton
Sunnyfields Organic Farm
Jacobs Gutter Lane
Totton
Southampton SO40 9FX
023 8087 1408
www.sunnyfields.co.uk

Surrey
Secretts Farm Shop
Hurst Farm
Chapel Lane
Milford, Godalming
Surrey GU8 5HU
01483 520 540
www.secretts.co.uk

Herefordshire
Ceci Paolo
The New Cook's Emporium
21 High Street
Ledbury
Herefordshire HR8 1DS
01531 632 976
www.cecipaolo.com

Hay Wholefoods & Deli
Lion Street
Hay-on-Wye,
Herefordshire HR3 5AA
01497 820 708

Edinburgh
Valvona and Crolla Ltd.
19 Elm Row
Edinburgh EH7 4AA
0131 556 6066
www.valvonacrolla.com

Harvey Nichols
Food Market
30-34 St Andrew Square
Edinburgh EH2 2AD
0131 524 8388
www.harveynichols.com

Glasgow
Grassroots
20 Woodlands Road
Glasgow G3 6UR
0141 353 3278
www.grassrootsorganic.com

Heart Buchanan
380 Byres Road
Glasgow G12 8AR
0141 334 7626
www.heartbuchanan.co.uk

Delizique Ltd.
66 Hyndland Street
Partick, Glasgow G11 5PT
0141 339 2000

Cork
Cork English Market
13-20 Grand Parade
Co. Cork
+ 353 21 492 4258

Dublin
La Corte
Epicurean Food Hall
36 Abby Street
Dublin
+ 353 1 873 4200

Farmers' Markets

London Farmers' Market
www.lfm.org.uk
020 7704 9659

National Association of
Farmers Markets
www.farmersmarkets.net

Index

The Authors would like to thank:

David Loftus, Mark Porter, Lesley McOwan, Fiona MacIntyre, Ian Heide, Matthew Armistead, Vashti Armit, Paul Barnes, Stephen Beadle, Sue Birtwistle, Daniel Bohan, Ronnie Bonetti, Daisy Boyd, Jonathan Conroy, Ros Ellis, Helio Fenerich, Susan Fleming, Imogen Fortes, Daisy Garnett, David Gleave, Ossie Gray, Gillian Hegarty, Theo Hill, Lynsey Hird, Jack Lewens, Sofia Manussis, Antonella Nieddu, Stephen Parle, Charles Pullan, Nina Raine, Theo Randall, Alan Rusbridger, Rosie Scott, David Stafford, Joseph Trivelli, Blanche Vaughan, Pirate Vereker, Ed Victor, Lucy Weigall, Joanne Wilkinson, Sian Wyn Owen, David MacIlwaine, Richard Rogers, The Staff of The River Cafe.

River Cafe Books

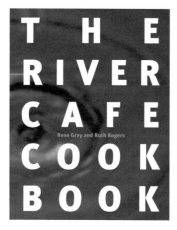

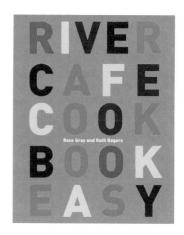

1 3 5 7 9 10 8 6 4 2 Text © Rose Gray and Ruth Rogers 2005. Rose Gray and Ruth Rogers have asserted their moral right to be identified as the authors of this work in accordance with the Copyright, Design and Patents Act 1988. All rights reserved. No part of this publication may be reproduced, stored in a retrieval system, or transmitted in any form by means, electronic, mechanical, photocopying, recording or otherwise, without the prior permission of the copyright owners. First published in the United Kingdom in 2005 by Ebury Press, Random House UK Ltd.20 Vauxhall Bridge Road, London SW1V 2SA; Random House Australia (Pty) Limited, 20 Alfred Street, Milsons Point, Sydney, New South Wales 2061, Australia; Random House New Zealand Limited, 18 Poland Road, Glenfield, Auckland 10, New Zealand; Random House (Pty) Limited, Endulini, 5A Jubilee Road, Parktown 2193, South Africa. Random House UK Limited Reg. No. 954009. www.randomhouse.co.uk.

A CIP catalogue record for this book is available from the British Library. Papers used by Ebury Press are natural, recyclable products made from wood grown in sustainable forests. ISBN:0091900328.

Printed and bound in Italy by Graphicom SRL

The Authors would like to thank:

David Loftus, Mark Porter, Lesley McOwan, Fiona MacIntyre, Ian Heide, Matthew Armistead, Vashti Armit, Paul Barnes, Stephen Beadle, Sue Birtwistle, Daniel Bohan, Ronnie Bonetti, Daisy Boyd, Jonathan Conroy, Ros Ellis, Helio Fenerich, Susan Fleming, Imogen Fortes, Daisy Garnett, David Gleave, Ossie Gray, Gillian Hegarty, Theo Hill, Lynsey Hird, Jack Lewens, Sofia Manussis, Antonella Nieddu, Stephen Parle, Charles Pullan, Nina Raine, Theo Randall, Alan Rusbridger, Rosie Scott, David Stafford, Joseph Trivelli, Blanche Vaughan, Pirate Vereker, Ed Victor, Lucy Weigall, Joanne Wilkinson, Sian Wyn Owen, David MacIlwaine, Richard Rogers, The Staff of The River Cafe.